Lost Restaurants

OF

THE OUTER BANKS

and Their Recipes

AMY POLLARD GAW

AMERICAN PALATE

Published by American Palate
A Division of The History Press
Charleston, SC
www.historypress.com

First published 2019

Manufactured in the United States

ISBN 9781467140812

Library of Congress Control Number: 2019932541

*This book is dedicated to the cooks and dishwashers,
whose names may never be printed.*

Contents

Acknowledgements

To choose these particular restaurants to remember was a difficult task; there were voluminous stories shared and photographs sent. Local photographers contributed, chefs emailed recipes and friends and fans recalled their favorite dining adventures.

The good folks at the Outer Banks History Center provided extensive documentation, including photos from the Roger Meekins, the Drew C. Wilson and the Aycock Brown Collections. Special thanks to Drew C. Wilson, who also helped me locate and identify images, as well as director Samantha Crisp and current and past staff members Stuart Parks, Tama Creef, Sarah Downing and Kaeli Schurr.

Melody Leckie and Mary Quidley generously shared their extensive and semi-secret stashes of historic food documents. Virginia Tillett invited me to her kitchen table to hear stories about Roanoke Island and her grandmother Lila Simmons's boardinghouse. Josie Meekins and Linwood Delroy Bowser sat on Josie's back porch with me until one of the chairs could no longer hold the weight of our conversation and provided at least one grandchild with a good laugh.

Ruth Toth met with me and shared Hatteras and Ocracoke Island food love stories, and several of the local librarians pointed me in the direction of old-school recipe books. John Railey wrote to me about Seafare, and Wanda Lewis shared about her mother's place, Nettie Pearl's. Lovey Selby talked me through traditional recipes. Kiki Kiousis fed me Greek appetizers after she modeled a full-length white leather coat from the Galleon and told hours of stories about her and her husband's memories of running Point Harbor Restaurant.

Friends reached out and memories were shared. Eugene Austin talked with me about his family, their cooking legacy, the Pea Island cookhouse and so much more. Dawn Taylor, Danny Couch, Susan West, Michael Peele, Dennis Robinson and Antoinette Mattingly shared stories, leads and context about Hatteras Island.

The Ocracoke Preservation Association, Leslie Lanier, Peter Vankevich, Wanda Midgette Beasley, Lisa Griggs, Kristine Kiousis, Eastern Albemarle Library System, Jamie Hope Anderson, Jim Trotman and so many others, thank you all for your help, you are all forever appreciated.

Thanks to the whole team at Arcadia Publishing and The History Press. Abigail Fleming and Jonny Foster, y'all are rockstars. To Kate Jenkins, my patient and kind book editor, go the biggest thanks and deepest gratitude for stamina, patience and mad editing skills. Big thanks to publisher and pal Beth Storie, who answered Kate Jenkins's email query for an author and referred her to me. Lifelong gratitude for Molly Perkins Harrison who has edited me for years and read this book, pre-press, and calmed my nerves.

Special thanks to Sweetie, John Gaw and our fuzzy, four-legged tuna, Vida, for group hugs and propping me up when the load got heavy. Enormous thanks, too, to Sweetie for sharing his forty-year historical perspective. Thanks to Mardee, Joe, Jacob, Garrett, Sharon (Mom), Richard (Dad), Karen (Godsend), Courtney, Cairo, Kalani, Angelo, Julie, Ellen, Dan and my entire family for loving and encouraging me.

Thanks to you, the reader, for picking this title. Hopefully, as you read this collection, you will remember a favorite eatery or two and enjoy cooking your way down memory lane.

Introduction

Jutting distinctly into the Atlantic Ocean, and backed by both brackish sounds and freshwater rivers, a series of narrow sandbars form what is known today as the Outer Banks of North Carolina. Located on the southeastern edge of the United States, this part of coastal Carolina has always been a food lover's paradise, even before there were restaurants.

The local estuary system surrounding the sandbars is the home to a variety of sea life, and there are few other places on earth where a culinarian can taste as many types of just-landed seafood as on the Outer Banks. Freshly caught and locally harvested have been buzzwords here for decades. Salty oysters, just-molted soft-shell crabs and sweet summertime shrimp are just a few of the most popular species and are all seasonally pulled from the surrounding saline-dense waters by equally salty local fishermen.

"You can't fool me on my seafood," said longtime Outer Banks cook, nutrition specialist and Manteo native Josie Meekins as she shook her head, "oh, no, you can't."

She is adamant, as are a host of other talented neighbors who have been in local restaurant kitchens for decades. They all have a similar refrain. Do not try to sell, or serve, them imported seafood—they know better. There are no substitutes for the flavors of seafood raised in the local waters. It is the *merroir*, the modern gourmands' write.

Native residents and longtime locals wax poetic about the consistent access to fresh-from-the-water ingredients, generously, and bravely, pulled

Fresh local seafood has always been a menu staple in Outer Banks restaurants. Pictured here is O'Neal's Seafood in Wanchese. *Photo by the author.*

from the water. Fisherman have always shared with their neighbors and bartered with the farmers. Food has always been community.

As luck would have it, many of the sharing and generous locals were also talented entrepreneurs and gifted cooks more than willing to serve these delicacies up on a plate, breakfast, lunch or dinner.

Whether the meals served at those lost restaurants were described as Southern, soul or coastal country, they were one and the same. Local specialties were skillfully prepared by dedicated cooks, and menus included predominately locally sourced ingredients. Seafood, pork, chicken, water fowl, venison, sweet potatoes, corn, collards and other greens were the key ingredients on the earliest menus, and that trend continues today, especially in the newer, farm-to-fork and sea-to-plate restaurants.

In this book, we explore the menus, legends and recipes of some of the most beloved, no longer operating, eateries of the Outer Banks.

Because each area of this rural, North Carolina resort is distinct, this book is sectioned into four geographic locales: 1) lower Currituck County; 2) the beaches of Dare and Currituck Counties; 3) Roanoke Island and the

Mainland of Dare County; and 4) Ocracoke Island, in Hyde County. Each area featured unique eateries, as well as personalities, that drew visitors back year after year.

THE BRIDGES

All three of the counties that make up the Outer Banks are connected by bridges, or bridges and a ferry ride. The bridges are all necessary and vital, and their mere construction did much to define industry and growth as well as carve out the present-day versions of neighborhoods.

Unless you are in a boat, there are only two ways to access the Outer Banks beaches from the mainland. The first is via Highway 158 in Currituck County, crossing over the 2.8-mile-long Wright Memorial Bridge.

The second is via Highway 64, driving over the Lindsay C. Warren Bridge, more commonly known as the Alligator River Bridge, then the William B. Umstead Bridge, the oldest operating bridge on the Outer Banks, which crosses the Croatan Sound and links Roanoke Island with mainland Dare County.

The 5.2-mile-long Virginia Dare Bridge is the new Highway 64 alternative to the Umstead Bridge and bypasses the town of Manteo entirely. This bridge was completed in 2002.

Either way, when arriving via Highway 64, you must drive over one more bridge, the Washington Baum Bridge, first built in 1928 and then rebuilt in 1994, before crossing the Melvin Daniels Bridge, then traversing the Nags Head–Manteo Causeway and arriving in the Whalebone Junction District of Nags Head. Phew. That's a lot of bridging.

The northern route, connecting Harbinger to Kitty Hawk, was originally a single-span bridge constructed of wood. Named for the flying duo from Ohio, the Wright Memorial Bridge passes over the Currituck Sound and was originally built in the early 1930s. At almost three miles long, the bridge resembled a boardwalk, and cars could cross at about twenty-five miles per hour, maximum speed.

At the time the bridge was built, the roads through Currituck, from the Virginia line south, were sparse, and the main two-lane road was lined with giant pines and ancient oaks. There were few retail businesses or restaurants; the main industry was agriculture. The road, now called NC 158, has been widened many times over the years, and all parts of Currituck now have four-lane, if not five-lane highways.

The Wright Memorial Bridge connects Currituck and Dare Counties. *Photo by the author.*

Traveling north on Highway 158 toward the Wright Memorial Bridge. Traffic on this day is sparse. This intersection is the busiest one on the Outer Banks, and traffic on Saturdays during season can be backed up for miles. *Photo by the author.*

When the first section of the modern-day Wright Memorial Bridge was built, it was a two-lane wonder and opened for traffic in 1966. That bridge is still being used and is the current eastbound span. What is now the westbound portion was opened in 1995. Today, there are two lanes on each span, and where eastbound traffic meets Route 12 in Kitty Hawk is one of the Outer Banks' most crucial and congested intersections.

Virginia Dare Trail, also known as the Beach Road, also known as NC Highway 12, was built in the early 1930s, not long after the original Wright Memorial Bridge was built, and runs parallel to the ocean from Kitty Hawk to Nags Head.

Wealthy white industrialists had constructed summer vacation homes on the northern barrier islands since the early to mid 1800s, bringing everything needed to build their seasonal homes by boat, then using mules to drag large packed containers to their final destinations. Development of NC 12 (the Beach Road) opened the door to construction of homes and businesses for those with more modest means. Even though trucks still had to cross that rickety wooden bridge to Kitty Hawk, building supplies could much more easily reach the newly purchased construction sites.

THE BOOM

Bridges were needed for any type of meaningful growth and especially if the Outer Banks wanted to promote tourism, which many residents did. Several northern beach developers initiated the Wright Memorial Bridge project and even incurred some of the expenses. The goal for some was hospitality; the goal for most was to bring visitors to the Outer Banks to buy property.

These links to the mainland increased visitor traffic in all three counties, and they also increased the need for services of all kinds. Overnight guests needed places to sleep, and they definitely needed places to eat.

It made sense that many of the first restaurants were adjoining boardinghouses and luxury hotels. They had captive audiences. Small fountain shops, burger bars, fried fish joints and family eateries soon followed. The larger hotels continued to feature fine dining and views of the waves. Their guests were, after all, economically enabled. Many hailed from larger cities and were used to certain standards of service. Waiters in jackets served multicourse meals, and guests dressed for dinner.

Family-style restaurants emerged in the 1960s and welcomed guests of all ages and parties of all sizes. Big baskets of lacey corn cakes, or cornbread, or corn griddlecakes appeared on the tables after everyone ordered. Sparks still ignite when diners reminisce about which fried corn appetizer was the best, meaning their favorite.

Business flowed and land development was gradually paced until the 1980s, when everything changed and the vacation real estate boom was full-on. That was the decade when sales folks introduced the tourists to time-share units. Beach rental properties became investments. Land was affordable, and developers bought large swaths to build what many still call McMansions, oversized rental homes, densely packed into contrived neighborhoods, active only three months a year, from Memorial Day until Labor Day.

According to advertisements, this development boom was for everyone. While visiting the Outer Banks, you could tune in to the local TV channels and learn, between commercials for local restaurants, just how to purchase a second home, one that not only paid for itself but also gave off income. If it seemed too good to be true, that is because it was, though it took a few years for investors to realize. Property values continued to rise; people continued to buy and sell and redecorate and build bigger piers and add pools and gourmet kitchens.

This was the golden age for property development, and it was the same for local restaurants. Real estate agents were selling high, and they, and industry associates, spent their money in the local economy, especially in the local restaurants. Tipping was big and re-tipping was even bigger, as many of the highly tipped would spend their evenings in late-night bars recirculating the money they had just pocketed.

Wine Spectator awards were garnished, cellars were enhanced and pricey bottles topped local wine lists. The '90s brought more of the same, and investors were sure it would never end. By the time the real estate market crashed in 2007, many Outer Bankers were house poor and the money just stopped circulating. Wine dinners dried up, holiday parties ceased and big tippers were usually from out of town, if at all. Regulars, even the pain in the butt variety, became special occasion diners; late-night bartenders served fewer and fewer drinks.

The recovery has been slow, and the Outer Banks eater has changed. Locals spend their money recovering from storms and have less money for eating out; when they do, they are looking for quantity as well as quality. Over the last decade, the majority of new restaurants on the Outer Banks

An advertisement for Penguin Isle in Nags Head touting its Wine Spectator awards and nightly sunset views. *Outer Banks Magazine*, 1993. *From the private collection of Melody Leckie.*

have been casual. Few have cloth napkins, let alone tablecloths. What is old is new again, and recycling, reusing and repurposing seems to be the local mantra. Corn cakes have even reappeared.

It is a little harder, though, to find fresh local seafood on menus these days. Fishing regulations have changed, and big food distributors now deliver imported product to the back door of most commercial kitchens. It is cheaper, they say. Not all restaurants have made the change, and it is often hard to tell who is serving what; be sure to ask if the seafood you are ordering is fresh and local.

THE CYCLE

There is an annual cycle that most restaurants on the Outer Banks recognize. Professional feeders on the Outer Banks work hard and fast for an intensely short period of time, and then many like to leave for a while, to relax, to play and to learn before coming back home and doing it all over again. As the area is a tourism mecca, the seven million visitors all like to eat at once and within the same, mostly summer, months.

For the enterprising food entrepreneur, the challenges of running a restaurant on the edge of the ocean have always been extensive, and that any owner made a go of it, for any amount of time, is commendable. While the seafood being caught is plentiful, getting it to the plate is no easy task and barriers abound: food distributers charge extra to make a delivery, the labor pool is shallow, storms and flooding occur without warning and the temporary, necessary, influx of seasonal tourism can mean three hundred for dinner one night and thirty the next.

While many eateries now stay open year-round, the unofficial restaurant calendar year begins vaguely around Valentine's Day, or maybe Easter, well, really around Memorial Day, depending on the weather, the economy, who you talk to and how much the business owner likes to travel. The Fourth of July brings the crowds, and then seven or eight weeks of hard crunch set in. Just when a good groove is established, the college kid helpers return to school, staffs become skeletal, and in a few more weeks, the money dries up, the lines disappear and everyone wonders what just happened and how it all stopped so quickly.

The fall and early winter brings the newly wed and the nearly dead, as the local saying goes. Families with pre-school age children and retirees enjoy the relaxed rental rates, and most seats in the restaurants are filled by two-tops. Larger tables are usually filled by fishermen and golfers instead of grandmas and cousins. Owners look at past receipts, food reps adjust expectations and seasonal closing dates are determined.

Even if this was not the original plan, many local entrepreneurs find that they are better off shutting their restaurant down until the visitors come back. Numbers, of the financial variety, are usually the leading reason for this practice. As it will, everything seems to find balance, and the restaurants that do stay open throughout the winter serving locals have a steady stream of business that would otherwise be spread too thin if all remained open.

All of this happens only if there is not a big storm that disrupts everything. Losing power can mean loss of business as well as loss of costly perishables.

Most businesses can only survive a hit or two; after a bigger flood, the cash flow often dries up before the sheetrock.

Despite all the challenges, it is in the spring that most budding restaurateurs open their own places, successful eateries expand and old favorites change their signs to reflect something new.

THE FOOD

Salt affects everything on the Outer Banks. A sweeping statement of the type I rarely make. This one is undeniable. The water from which we harvest and the land on which we grow are injected and infused with a salinity that flavors and resonates in everything we humans are able to eat or drink. The oyster is the sea, the soft-shell is the sound, the grape is the wind and the collards are the composted seashells of long ago times.

Devil Shoal oysters, from Heather and Fletcher O'Neal in Ocracoke, are briny examples of locally sourced seafood. *Photo by the author.*

Most of us are familiar with the word *terroir*, especially when used at a wine tasting. Depending on the soil, the sun, the drainage and a myriad of other variables, a sense of place is recognized by a refined palate. You might recognize this tasty phenomenon locally, like in an Ocracoke fig or a Knotts Island peach. It is easy to transition that same sense of place to the water and taste the merroir. A crab slough oyster tastes like none other, and that is because an oyster tastes almost exactly like the water in which it lives.

THE HISTORY

The majority of restaurants here today, on the Outer Banks, in rural North Carolina, only exist because of tourism. The local population could not support them all. Most restaurateurs admit that locals are not even their target diners, and they market, and price, their menus accordingly. A handful of eateries do still cater to locals and thrive on the added boost of revenue in the summer months.

It wasn't always this way. The Outer Banks didn't always have restaurants.

Exploring the concept of paying for a plate of food in this area reveals that the word *restaurant* is a fairly modern one, and before the 1960s, most local eateries were called shops, cafés, lodges or diners. For decades, from the turn of the century until the 1960s, there were villages on the Outer Banks where you could purchase a meal only at a boardinghouse or a waterfowl hunting lodge.

Savvy entrepreneurs like Lila Simmons and Cordelia Wise opened boardinghouses on Roanoke Island and provided seasonal meals for traveling black workers and visitors. Waterfowl hunters ate what was served up by the local camp cooks in Currituck, often tucked into thermoses and wrapped in paper, eaten midday, in the field or in duck blinds on top of the sounds.

Many locals, especially on Hatteras Island, rarely paid to have anyone cook for them, even when given the opportunity. Few still do, save the occasional community dinner or fundraising fish fry. Restaurants south of Oregon Inlet found it incredibly challenging to survive on local trade alone, and most eateries along the southern beaches relied almost exclusively on hungry tourists.

When I first moved to the Outer Banks, in the mid-eighties, there were only a handful of eateries up and down the entire beach, high-end to grab-

and-go. It was easy, then, to name, from memory, every restaurant on the newer, main road, called the Bypass, as well as the ones that lined the Beach Road. These days, there are almost four hundred restaurants, independent and franchised, operating in Dare, Currituck and Hyde Counties.

Workers have become owners, and their children now tend bars. The population continues to increase, and new restaurants open weekly. Legacy restaurants, like Owens Restaurant in Nags Head and Blue Point in Duck, continue to serve new and returning guests. Things have changed, yet they are very much the same.

Lower Currituck County

Point Harbor, Harbinger, Powells Point, Jarvisburg

The northern access to the Outer Banks, over the Wright Memorial Bridge, takes you through Currituck County, specifically an area referred to now as lower Currituck. Now an active area for commerce, this used to be an agricultural haven, and farmers grew acres of food in the loamy, fertile soil.

Sweet potatoes and collards were on winter tables, and peaches, figs and local berries dominated the summertime farm stands that dotted the two-lane road. These crops are still grown, though the road is wider and the individual stands have been replaced by grander ones that are supplemented with produce from surrounding farms as well as offloaded from big food trucks.

The county is surrounded by water, and fishing and waterfowl hunting have always been legacies. Venison, goose and the daily catch were longtime community table staples until government regulations restricted the sale of locally hunted meats. Fish is still a good bet, in season, and landed amid heavy regulation.

Corn has always been a vital crop and continues to be in Currituck, along with soybeans and canola; most crops, however, are not grown for local consumption. Thankfully, some small farms are still operating, and more young people are actively engaging with their food sources and more soil is being tilled every season.

Currituck also is home to the Bennowitz families' Weeping Radish Brewery and Charcuterie, the first microbrewery in the state, as well as

Above: Locally grown may peas are hulled by both human hand and this handy machine. Grandy Greenhouse and Farm Market. *Photo by the author.*

Left: Summer harvest from a Currituck roadside market. *Photo by the author.*

Tractors were, and still are, a common sight on both major and back roads of Currituck. *Photo by the author.*

Sanctuary Vineyards, where the Wright family makes wine from home-grown grapes and not just the scuppernong. My own business, Outer Banks SeaSalt, the first modern documented sea salt company in the state, is also located in Currituck.

Post-1960s, more than one author referred to this area as the Outer Banks country. That's why we included these memorable restaurants, to celebrate the country side of the Outer Banks.

NETTIE PEARL'S PLACE—POWELL'S POINT

Country cooking was what most people called the food served by Nettie Pearl Lewis at her tiny eatery in Currituck. Just a few minutes up the road from the Wright Memorial Bridge, Nettie Pearl's was a go-to stop for both travelers to the beach and locals driving to Norfolk or beyond.

On the "Outer Banks Vintage Scrapbook" Facebook page, Linda Crumpler Pearce remembered,

My most unforgettable lunch there happened on a cold, snowy day. I was on the way to Elizabeth City from Manteo with my friend Dianne Tillett. Weather and roads got so bad we turned around to come home, but took time to stop at Nettie Pearl's for lunch. Best beef stew and home-made yeast rolls I've ever eaten! And that coconut cake was also unforgettable.

Nettie Pearl's served breakfast, lunch and dinner, six days a week. On the seventh day, the sign outside proclaimed SHUT UP ON SUNDAYS, much to the delight of many who still remember the exact wording.

Nettie's daughter Wanda Lewis recalled, "She did everything herself in the tiny restaurant. There were three booths, three tables and three counter seats, and when the restaurant was overflowing, people would take their plates into the yard and dine on swing set seats or venture into our house, next door to the restaurant."

She laughed, "Sometimes people I had never seen before in my life would come in a little, tiny, house that we lived in beside the restaurant and sat and ate their meals in the house while talking to my grandma, and me just sitting there looking at them!"

Customers remember pitching in and love to share stories about how they helped. Wanda recalled, "When she was so busy, people would get in the kitchen and they would wash the dishes and scald them in the big old stainless steel sink with the heavy duty heating element that was required by the health department in those days. They would help her dry the dishes and keep on keepin' on."

Nettie Pearl's standards were high, her friends say, and she bought seafood only from folks she knew and trusted. She made what she wanted and she also honored requests; she cooked a leg of lamb with homemade mint jelly every Friday night for neighbors from up north because they asked.

Nettie Pearl Ballance Lewis was a risk taker. Nettie's daughter Wanda shared,

She told me the story, right before she died, of how she got on top of Wright Memorial on that motorcycle. She said her and her boyfriend were flying across the rickety wooden Wright Memorial Bridge from Currituck to Dare County. She said she was scared to death. He wouldn't slow down and the cops started chasing them.…He flew down the highway and rode the bike up on top of the hill.

Nettie Pearl washing dishes in her tiny kitchen in Powells Point; customers often stepped in to help. *Courtesy of Wanda Lewis.*

The officers arrived at the foot of the Wright Memorial and were all getting out of their cars and proceeding to climb their way up the hill by foot. He told her to straighten up her hair, fix herself and smile! He took her picture, told her that it was a memory she would never forget! I don't know the name of the boyfriend, nothing is written on the picture at all. I do know that's a true story, there was some other old-timers that used to talk about her riding the motorcycle with this fella.

Nettie Pearl was well known outside of the area, too. There were articles in the *New York Times* and the *Washington Post* about the little place called Nettie Pearl's, a must-stop destination on the way to the Outer Banks. Traveling writers shared stories of eating chicken and dumplings and fried seafood and giant slices of pie.

People loved her pies. Unfortunately, she left behind no known written recipes. Said Wanda, "Mama was a sling and dump cook, no recipes ever, she would always say to me 'you better watch me make this, because one day you will want to know how and I don't know how to tell you. You have to watch me.' I wished I'd listened to her all those years."

Her sling and dump technique was confirmed by many who said things similar to Eva Bilderback, who recalled, "She made so many at one time, I remember her having a huge pot on the stove boiling with a mixture permeating chocolate. While it was boiling, she would dump frozen vanilla ice cream in it and continue on."

Chrissie Ball shared,

Nettie Pearl Ballance Lewis, owner and operator of Nettie Pearl's, as a young adventurer, perched on her boyfriend's Harley-Davidson. *Courtesy of Wanda Lewis.*

I have two recipes Nettie dictated to me one night while I sat at her counter. I used to stay for a couple hours when I lived in Dare County back in the late 70's. She was like a second mama. I used to love the vegetable plate of sides: potato salad, cole slaw, collard greens, fruit salad, cucumber salad, apple sauce—with hush puppies and rolls. Also her delicious vegetable soup! I loved all the pies of course, especially the million-dollar pie. I don't have quantities.

Nettie's Cucumber Salad

Slice cucumbers and onions. Place in bowl. Sprinkle thoroughly with salt and put in refrigerator overnight. When ready to make, pour vinegar over cucumber slices and onions. Drain. Fold in a container of sour cream. Season and chill.

Nettie's Fruit Salad

1 can fruit cocktail
Bananas, apples, sliced peaches, chunk pineapple
Raisins, pears and a tiny bit of celery or miniature marshmallows

Drain all canned fruit well. Stir in a large size Cool Whip and chill.

POINT HARBOR GRILL

Point Harbor

One of the most resilient restaurant locations in lower Currituck is the Point Harbor Restaurant and its future iterations.

When heading to the Outer Banks on the northernmost route, the road traverses a small town in Currituck County called Point Harbor. It is the last town you drive by before you reach the Wright Memorial Bridge. On the north side of the road, perched on the edge of the Currituck Sound, is a restaurant that began its life as Point Harbor Restaurant. Currently operating as Masala Bay, an Indian restaurant, the location features a small marina that is popular with Kitty Hawk and Southern Shores diners with access to boats.

"When they announced the building of the new span on the bridge, we knew it was time to sell," said former owner Kiki Kiousis. "We would lose all our parking and the easy access to the restaurant." Kiki and her husband, Yperochos, otherwise known as Perry, were the second owners of the popular eatery. Ruth and Walton Griggs were the original owners and built the restaurant in 1945. The Kiousis family took over in 1969, shortly after visiting the Outer Banks for the first time.

The original owners of Point Harbor Restaurant, Ruth and Walton Griggs, built a successful business and knew the value of their location and their staff—they also knew how to market. They told their story on matchbooks: "Fine Food, Carefully Prepared. Steaks, Chicken and Seafood," the diner-red covers proclaimed. The Griggs had two daughters, Margie and Mollie, and ran the restaurant as a family-friendly establishment.

They sold the property to Perry and Kiki, who had some food experience in Pittsburgh. Said Kiki,

Ruth and Walton Griggs, the original owners of Point Harbor Restaurant. *Outer Banks Vintage Scrapbook.*

We had a good customer at our hotdog shop in Pittsburgh who had a place in Nags Head, near the pier. He said since we were from Greece, from the beautiful Mediterranean, we would like it here. He gave us a deal for two weeks and so we took the kids and the babysitter and went to Nags Head.

All we saw was the sand. We came straight to the beach. Maybe a couple hundred houses, a dozen or so restaurants. Perry said we should buy property here because we couldn't buy anything in Pittsburgh.

First, we looked in Norfolk. As we drove back over the bridge, this was in August, we were passing the Wright Brothers Bridge and we passed a small, nice restaurant that was packed. I saw a parking lot full of cars and told Perry we should find a restaurant like this. Well, the Norfolk property wasn't right.

So, the next day, Perry went to Robert Young Realty at Avalon Pier and asked him if there were any restaurants for sale. He said there is a restaurant across the bridge in Point Harbor. He called Mr. Griggs right then and Mr. Griggs said he would sell it right now for $225,000, as is. He would take $5,000 down and finance the rest. We made the agreement without even seeing the inside of the place. Perry was a carpenter, we *thought we could just fix whatever needed to be fixed. We had no idea how bad everything was.*

We had a longtime waitress who asked if we knew what we just bought. She answered her own question with "a big headache." She was right. We closed on the property in November and as soon as we opened, the health department came in and took the "A" [rating] from the wall and said we had to shut down because we didn't have a septic tank.

Nick Kiousis, Kiki's son, shared,

Seeing these photos and reading these comments bring back some great memories! I still have an original Point Harbor Restaurant menu. Mom & Dad owned it from November '69 to December '81. When Dad tried to open for business his first day the health inspector showed up and shut him down. "Flush your toilets and come outside, Mr. Perry." They went out to the waterside of the store and my dad watched in horror as the pipe coming out of the sound bank spewed out toilet water! That's right, the grill had been using the Currituck Sound as a septic tank for 25 years! "But they were the biggest damn crabs you've ever seen!" Dad said.

"Well, you can imagine what that meant," expanded Kiki,

It cost $24,000 to put in that septic and we had a lot of help making it happen. A nice customer drew the plans for no charge. Mo Griggs, the first cousin of the original owner, talked to the bank and they guaranteed us a loan. Robert Young let us use his commission on the sale for start-up inventory until we could pay him back. We had a lot of help.

We needed a place to live and Mr. Shelby Hines helped us build our first home. He sold us the lot in Southern Shores for $5,000 and that included a membership to Duck Woods County Club. It was challenging to run the restaurant and build the house. My uncle came and got our boys and took them to Greece for the summer and that is how we built the house.

This was a good community for us, even though there were not many other Greeks. Alice Sykes at the Sea Ranch had a right hand woman who was Greek....and Ted Cotsimopolous who owned the Bonanza Cottage Court. That was about it.

We started having Greek Night once a year, at Christmas time. It was always a big hit. The ladies dressed up and we made a big buffet of Greek specialties. All kinds of Greek food. Everyone came.

Kiki's eyes twinkled as she explained about how the ladies, and the men, dressed up, and everyone was a little more fashion aware that one night a year.

The rest of the time, we cooked seafood dinners. We had shrimp, oysters, fish, crabcakes and this wonderful lacey cornbread. We would get all our seafood from Billy and Judy Beasley at Billy's Seafood. We would pick it up or they would deliver, usually 3 times a week. We had one food distributor and that was Jeannette's. That's where we got it all. The prices we charged were fair, the fried shrimp was $6.95 and we had $1.50 breakfasts.

Wanda Midgette Beasley, now owner of her own restaurant and catering operation in Currituck, BJ's Carolina Café and Wanda's Creative Catering, recalled, "I learned so much that I didn't even know I was learning about food service from my early years there."

Kiki Kiousis and her husband, Perry, were owner-operators of Point Harbor Restaurant. *Photo by Perry Kiousis.*

The Point Harbor Restaurant dining room, overlooking the Currituck Sound, where thousands of hungry patrons happily ate baskets of hot buttery corn cakes. *Photo by Perry Kiousis.*

Billy's Seafood, in Colington, has been supplying fresh seafood to Outer Banks restaurants for over fifty years. *Photo by the author.*

She also reminisced about working with local cooks Dusty Brown and Lizzie Dough:

> *They tossed in a bit of this and a bit of that and always a handful of SUGAR! I recall ever so fondly them cutting up cabbage for cole slaw and—get ready for this—mixing it! mayonnaise, sugar and vinegar, using their bare arms as a paddle or spoon to mix it up. They'd have a huge deep pan and have their arm all the way down to their arm pits mixing that good old yummmmmy cole slaw with their arms and hands—no gloves, no anti germ hand wash and we all survived.*

Because the first and second owners employed the same women to do the cooking, many of the recipes, such as the famous corn cakes, happily continued. The staff was invaluable to both the first owners, the Griggs, as well as the Kiousis family. Kiki said, "We had a great staff. We asked the former staff to stay and most did. We were open for ten years until the state contacted us and said they were taking our land for the new bridge. That's when Perry came up with the idea for Stack 'em High."

Nick Kiousis added, "I remember as a young boy running through the kitchen on busy Friday nights when the place was packed with customers. I'd dart in between the girls cooking on the line, stick my hand into the shrimp pan and grab a handful of fresh, fried greentails, then shove them into my mouth. The ladies would holler: 'Go on now, they's for customers!'"

Kiki's Greek Night Moussaka

3 onions, chopped
2 pounds ground round steak, or ground lamb
¾ cup tomato paste
½ cup red wine
2 teaspoons cinnamon
1 teaspoon nutmeg
3 tablespoons fresh parsley
Dash of garlic salt
Dash of salt
Dash of pepper
3 medium eggplants
½ cup olive oil
½ cup bread crumbs

6 large eggs
1 ½ cups grated Romano cheese
2½ cups milk, heated
2 tablespoons flour
¼ pound butter, melted

Sauté onion until it becomes transparent. Brown the meat slowly. Dilute tomato paste with water and wine; add spices. Mix tomato mixture into meat and simmer, covered, until all liquid is absorbed. Cut eggplants lengthwise into ¼-inch slices. Sprinkle with flour and fry in olive oil until brown.

In a 9 × 13 pan, sprinkled with bread crumbs, set a layer of eggplant. Beat the egg whites slightly and add to meat mixture. Sprinkle 3 tablespoons of breadcrumbs on eggplant. Place some of the meat mixture over the eggplant. Cover with some grated Romano cheese and cover with more meat until all the eggplant is used. Beat the egg yolks and add to hot milk. Add 2 tablespoons flour and grated cheese—heat thoroughly. Pour this mixture over the top layer of eggplant. Pour melted butter over the top. Bake at 350 degrees for about 35 minutes. Serves 12–14.

Author's note: Recipe directions printed as provided. You might want to substitute your own béchamel recipe for the technique listed.

Point Harbor Restaurant was a popular spot for gathering locals together, and photographer Aycock Brown often used the location as a backdrop for advertisements to visit the Outer Banks. *Photo by Aycock Brown, courtesy Outer Banks History Center.*

POTS ON 'N' KITCHEN

Harbinger

Family owned and operated Pots On 'N' Kitchen restaurant was located on Highway 158 on the Currituck mainland in Harbinger and was a planned destination when heading to and from the beaches. It also was popular with working folks who lived and worked nearby.

One of the many reasons Pots On, as locals called it, was famous was the corn cakes. Oh my goodness. They were remarkable. I haven't had all the corn cakes folks in this book rave about, but I did taste these and they were absolutely cravable. Those golden treats were complimentary, hot, sweet and griddle cooked with love. After a slather of butter, or not, you could hear the moans in the dining room. Yes, corn cakes really did this to people, and yes, we are sharing the recipe.

Ginger Bowden and sisters Katherine Johnson and Joyce Hines opened the restaurant in 1987, after running the vegetable stand on the same property. None had cooked professionally, but they knew how to feed people and they knew how to do business. They made all their dishes from scratch and worked long hours, often with sleeping children tucked away in the dining room as they washed the dishes and closed for the night.

They knew about feeding people, and they were really good at it. Getting food in a hungry customer alleviated a lot of discontent, and those corn cakes did the trick. Smart women.

Patricia B. Mitchell wrote on her website, foodhistory.com, in 2004, "We enjoyed our dinner in the family-oriented eatery with the 'funny' name." Mitchell went on to say that she was told that it was a family saying that meant, "Please come in and eat with us. The pot of food on the kitchen stove is ready and available."

It truly was a family operation. After a few years of serving thousands of plates of food, Ginger and Joyce released the restaurant reins to Ginger's brother Walter and his wife, Penni. Their daughters and spouses, Sherry and Hagan Fischlschweiger and Tanya and Bill Neelan, were next on board. They closed for business in September 2007.

When I prospected the restaurant a few years after it closed, in search of my own location, I saw that the mural of the property was still on the wall. Bill was showing me the property and told me that they were hoping to have it removed some day, though no one was quite sure what to do with it or how to get it done. At that time, the space was being

Right: The Pots On 'N' Kitchen sign, several months after it closed for service for good, in 2007. *Photo by the author.*

Below: A mural inside the Pots On 'N' Kitchen building. The subject is the restaurant building and surrounding property. The owner of the building still hopes to some day remove it and save it. *Photo by the author.*

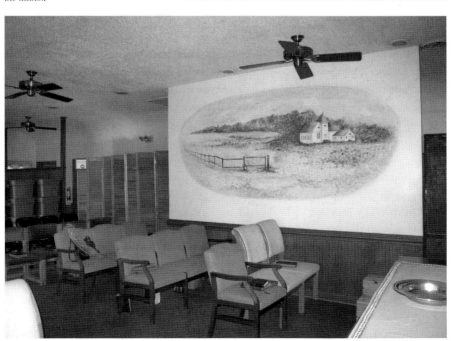

rented to a local congregation and they had church services inside twice a week.

The restaurant was best known for home cooking, and it always offered a large selection of vegetable sides to accompany homey entrées such as fried shrimp, fried oysters, pork chops, meatloaf and fried fresh fish. The food was comforting and Southern and soulful and all the words that made people plan their day around eating there.

Customers had their favorite dishes, but the most commonly remembered item wasn't even on the menu. It was the complimentary basket of sweet, just griddled corn cakes.

Pots On Corn Cakes

Eat them with your fingers, eat them with a fork. Add butter. Refuse butter. Add syrup. Deny syrup. There is no wrong way to eat these. Serve them in the summer with sliced tomatoes, cucumber-onion salad and grilled fish. Serve them for breakfast in the winter with eggs and salty meat—country ham or thick, smoked bacon.

Contributed by Jamie Hope Anderson, as shared by a staff member.

4 eggs
1 12-ounce can corn
1 pint milk
2 cups sugar
2 cups flour
1 tablespoon vanilla
1 cup cornmeal

No instructions were provided, but Jamie mixed everything together and cooked the batter like pancakes. These can be made tiny or large. Eat them with a fork or with your fingers. Add butter when hot. Add any other topping as desired. Suggestions: maple syrup, honey.

Northern Beaches, Currituck County and Dare County

Corolla, Duck, Southern Shores, Kitty Hawk, Kill Devil Hills, Colington, Nags Head

The Northern Beaches, in this book, mean all the sandy beach communities north of Oregon Inlet and east of Roanoke Island. All have access to the ocean, except for Colington, which has access to the ocean via Kill Devil Hills; it is often considered part of Kill Devil Hills, but it is really in unincorporated Dare County.

The southern towns of the Northern Beaches—Nags Head, Kill Devil Hills, Colington and Kitty Hawk—are mixed-use yet old-school beach communities. Vintage cottages, art centers, neighborhoods and fishing piers are intertwined with fast-food restaurants, casual independent eateries and a variety of other businesses. Planned multiuse paths now line most of the Beach Road and planners hope these efforts will help the Outer Banks become more visitor friendly.

As you drive north on Highway 12, you sense a more new-school approach to life, though not necessarily a modern one. The first town north of Kitty Hawk is Southern Shores, a planned community deeply entrenched in a maritime forest. Retirees and young families make up the majority of the population, and the town is home to the Outer Banks' only country club, called Duck Woods.

A few of the remaining flat-top houses are representative of a nouveau architecture style, popular when the town was just a village. Most Southern Shores neighborhood homes are populated by residents with a bit more in their housing budget than their southern neighbors.

Above: Beach accesses like this one at Eighth Street in Kill Devil Hills define the beach road in the oceanfront communities. *Photo by the author*.

Left: Storms, hurricanes, erosion and shifting sands present unique challenges to Outer Banks entrepreneurs. *Photo by the author*.

Duck, in Dare County, and Corolla, in Currituck County, are the next two towns to the north on this ribbon of road known as NC Highway 12. The differences in the style and scale of architecture become apparent, and you begin to realize that these northern communities are made up of gargantuan rental cottages, beach culture–oriented retail shops and more than a fair share of wine and steamed seafood bars.

Said Beth Storie, owner of One Boat Guides,

> *It's amazing to look back and see how quickly the Corolla and Duck dining scenes changed in the first half of the 1990s. By the summer of 1996, there were 11 restaurants in Corolla and 12 in Duck! When you consider that the road into Corolla had only been open to the public for 12 years by that time, you begin to imagine the exponential and fast change that took place in that area.*

BUDDHALICIOUS

Corolla

BuddhaLicious, a hip sushi-sake bar in Corolla was short-lived but long in flavors. *Photo by the author.*

This hip, recently closed, little joint was located in an unassuming strip mall on the east side of Highway 12 in Corolla. Its extensive list of sake and jizake (small-batch sake) was a new concept to the Outer Banks, and many guests learned life lessons about pairing these beverages with food from around the globe with the chef and owner, Todd Bryant.

The clever adaptation of the restaurant space was both cool and intimate. You wanted to return. Enhanced by blue lights and a corrugated metal bar base, the atmosphere was hip and moody. The cool tones could have been stark; instead, the space was intimate and just roomy enough, and the black booths presented as both artsy modern and Asian classic.

Japanese-inspired fish prints covered a corner sushi booth, and a small bar lined with sake and jazake made for its own artful installation.

BuddhaLicious's sushi rolls were clever. The Korean Country Tacos were made with generous chunks of bulgogi, braised short ribs, tucked into corn tortillas and topped with house-made kimchi, queso fresco and fresh cilantro.

The children's menu even followed the theme and featured Veggie Springrolls, Sweet & Sour Chicken Bowl, Fried Rice Bowl, Beef Lo Mein or even a Chicken Finger Sushi Roll.

BARRIER ISLAND INN

Duck

The first sit-down, fancy-ish restaurant in Duck was Barrier Island Inn. Well, as fancy as you can get with a Skee-Ball game in the corner. Duck became an independent town in 2002, and Barrier Island Inn now operates as Sunset Grill and Raw Bar.

Thanks to Chef Q Kathleen Derks, for sharing these recipes:

The Barrier Island Inn peanut butter chocolate cheesecake was made by a woman named Pat Heath who was making desserts for a lot of the restaurants on the Outer Banks at the time. She stopped doing it because she and her husband, Chuck, went on to open the Outer Banks Potato Chip Factory. She gave me the recipe so that I could continue making them for a Barrier Island Inn.

Complimentary Clam Dip

John Lancaster and Paul Shaver, who went on to open Black Pelican, understood that feeding people immediately helped ease everyone's nerves, so, they offered a bit of snack: house-made clam dip.

½ cup chopped canned clams, drained
1 pound cream cheese, room temperature
¼ cup chopped black olives
2 tablespoons chopped green onion
1 tablespoon Worcestershire sauce

Fold all ingredients together and serve with your favorite cracker.

The Sunset Grille, originally built and operated as Barrier Island Inn, in Duck. *Photo by the author.*

Peanut Butter Chocolate Cheesecake

Crust

5 cups graham cracker crumbs
½ cup sugar
¼ cup butter, melted

Filling

3 pounds cream cheese
2 cups sugar
6 eggs
1 cup sour cream
2 cups chocolate chips
2 cups Reese's peanut butter chips

Ganache

4 cups chocolate chips
2 cups heavy cream

Bring all filling ingredients to room temperature before starting. Prepare two 9-inch springform pans with a crust of crumbs, sugar and about a quarter cup of melted butter (just enough so that it sticks together when pressed hard). Cream together cream cheese and sugar. Add eggs one at a time. Do not over beat (this will make the cheesecake tough if you do, so don't). Fold in sour cream and divide batter into two parts. Microwave chocolate chips and whisk into one half of the batter. Microwave peanut butter chips and whisk into the other half of the batter. Pour in half peanut butter and then half chocolate batter into each springform. Use a skewer or a knife to swirl the two flavors together. Place the cheesecakes into an unheated oven. Turn the oven to 500 degrees and let them cook for 15 minutes. Reduce the temperature to 250 degrees and let them cook for one hour, then turn off the oven and let cheesecakes sit in the off oven for one hour. Take out of the oven and let cool on the counter for one hour. Then place in the refrigerator until completely cooled.

For the ganache, place chocolate chips in a food processor and heat heavy cream to a near boil in the microwave. Pour the heavy cream over the chips and blend until smooth. Pour over top of the cheesecakes and return to the refrigerator to chill

FROM THE COVER OF THE ORIGINAL BARRIER ISLAND INN MENU

A Brief History of Duck, *by Robert Furr*

Though historians document inhabitants in the Duck area as early as the mid 1700's it wasn't until 1909 that Lloyd A. Toler, first postmaster to the village established an office here, and named the village Duck, for the abundance of waterfowl that inhabited the area. Known simply as North Banks prior to this time, the tiny community consisted of a mere handful of

Barrier Island Inn was a full-service restaurant located on the sound in Duck. The menu was designed by the prolific local graphic artist Bob Furr and featured a variety of entrées, including fresh, locally caught game fish. *Author's collection.*

families, who made their living either fishing, hunting or as lifesavesmen, at the lifesaving station at nearby Corolla. Duck's most famous resident, Dan Tate, is credited as the Wright Brothers right-hand assistant on their work here (no pun intended), and was on hand December 17, 1903 when first flight was achieved. Members of the Tate family still reside in Duck today, as do relatives of many of the original families first inhabiting the area.

In the early 1900's wildfowl was hunted commercially and longnets were employed to fish the sound, both yielding abundant catches, and lucrative incomes. Loaded on steam driven freighters from Elizabeth City, local seafood and wildfowl was taken there, then shipped to New York and Baltimore, where eagerly awaiting purveyors turned Duck's finest export into high dollar profits. Packing houses were constructed on pilings out in the sound. Fishing piers and hunt clubs dotted the great Currituck's shore line. Summers saw bass fishermen testing our waters, winter brought the elite duck hunter from the northern and Midwestern states to hunt the famous Currituck Sound employing locals for guides, and rewarding them handsomely for their services.

But, nothing lasts forever. By the 1930's government controls had banned the sale of wildfowl, and the fishing got scarce. No longer did the great Currituck yield to her residents the lucrative means of trade. Soon the freighters stopped coming, and Duck locals were forced to seek income by other means.

At the Barrier Island Inn, we feel a responsibility as Duck's first restaurant and public gathering to provide for our clientele not only fine food and drink, but as well, a brief insight into what makes our community so special and cherished by its inhabitants. For those interested in further information, we recommend local historian David Stick's book, The Outer Banks of North Carolina, *available at most local bookstores and information centers. To our local friends, we dedicate our restaurant to you, extend our sincerest wishes that you consider yourselves an important part of our establishment, and further hope that we might, as representatives of our community, reflect the friendliness, warmth and hospitality that lies at the very heart of you, the good people of Duck.*

CAROLINA BLUE

Southern Shores

Chip Smith and Tina Vaughan, the owners of Carolina Blue in Southern Shores, might be the only former Outer Banks restaurateurs who have ever been reviewed by Pete Wells of the *New York Times*. This was not their Southern Shores restaurant, but the one after, called the Simone, which sounds deliciously like the place locals and visitors to the OBX came to adore.

From the June 3, 2014 review by food writer Pete Wells:

The chef Chip Smith and his wife, Tina Vaughn, moved to New York in 2012 after shutting their restaurant in North Carolina, but the Simone, which they opened in November, doesn't feel like a transplanted Southern flower. It is a classic Manhattan restaurant that seems to have emerged on East 82nd Street fully formed out of a time capsule sealed in the last century.

When you call the restaurant, which is the only way to reserve one of its 11 tables, Ms. Vaughn will write your name in something called a "book," holding an implement known as a "pen." She applies the same antique tool to the menu, which she writes out in cursive and photocopies each time Mr. Smith changes it.

If you were designing a dish to go viral on Instagram, you'd start by ruling out flounder, which has the must-see quotient of a "Matlock" marathon on TBS. The fish is a favorite of Mr. Smith's, who served me two flounder dishes that rank among the best seafood I've tasted this year. In late winter, he rolled juicy, big-flaked fillets around a mousse of flounder and black truffle flecks; I would have burrowed into it until spring if I hadn't also wanted to eat the whole thing. The flounder's cold-weather swaddling disappeared a few weeks ago, and a jaunty new May outfit appeared: a golden sheet of bread crumbs speckled with fresh green herbs on top of the fish, a platform of crushed, minted favas below.

Chef Chip Smith with sous chef Phongrit "Pok" Choeichom. *Photo by Jim Trotman.*

Laura Martier remembers Carolina Blue being her favorite restaurant for a multitude of reasons. Her daughter, Lucy, worked there when she was very young. Said Martier,

They taught her how to eat, how to use glassware and silverware. She peeled endless piles of garlic and anything else the sous chef Pok did not want to do. She learned how to dine there and always ordered soup to start, filet medium rare. Chip was always making her a dessert with some sort of spun sugar dome over it! I loved to hear Lucy order there. Every single thing I ate there seemed perfect to me at the time.

She went on:

Chip's food was just flawless in my opinion. The menu was always fresh and adventurous, rabbit, organ meat, homemade pate, foie gras. I used to swoon over Chip's homemade gnocchi. Tina's choice of wines were always perfectly paired with what Chip was cooking and I learned so much from

her about old world wines. She knew exactly what I liked and always just poured for me. They treated everyone like a friend and had their hands on every table. I had amazing birthday dinner there where they set a table up in the middle of the entire room. You wanted to get dressed up to go there; I always wore lipstick.

Martier is a singer and performing artist and was especially sentimental as she shared, "They closed the restaurant down for a night to cater my jazz CD release post concert reception at Roanoke Island Festival Park. What a classy swanky time."

Former sous chef turned restaurateur Phongkrit Pok Choeichom said this about the couple:

They taught me a lot, and showed me the way of how food should be prepared and tasted. I started working with them day one till they moved to Chapel Hill. She was like my second mom, they both took me under their wings and treated me like family. The best memory I have with them was going to NYC to do a James Beard house dinner.

This was exactly what the Outer Banks was fortunate enough to have for just a few short but delicious years. Visit the Vaughans for dinner in their new place, the Simone, located in New York City.

Puree of Chestnut Soup

¼ cup chopped leeks
1 ½ pounds peeled and roasted chestnuts (reserve ¼ pound for garnish)
3 cups chicken stock
1 ½ cups heavy cream
Salt
White pepper
Chives
Crème fraiche

Trim leeks of all green; reserve white parts and clean thoroughly. Chop leeks and sweat until translucent. Add chestnuts and cover with chicken stock. Bring to a boil and reduce to simmer for 25–30 minutes. Puree until smooth and add cream, salt and white pepper to taste. Strain through chinois, checking consistency and seasoning.

Serve in warm bowls with garnish of chopped chives, reserved chopped chestnuts and a dollop of crème fraîche.

SOUTHERN BEAN COFFEE SHOP

Southern Shores and Kitty Hawk

Eric Gardner was the co-owner of the first coffee house on the northern Outer Banks. In the late nineties, with his partner and first wife, Garnette Guyton Coleman, he carved out a caffeine-friendly niche in the Market Place Shopping Center in Southern Shores.

The laid-back shop provided an easy hangout for locals of all ages, and the duo offered a variety of healthy wraps and breakfast treats. One of the most popular was called a Happy Wrap—a large specialty tortilla shell smeared

This photo was taken inside Southern Bean and was shared by Eric's widow, Tina Gardner. It was captured by an unknown guest, on April 20, one of his favorite days of the year. *Courtesy of Tina Gardner.*

with peanut butter, yogurt and honey, topped with banana and crunchy-sweet granola. The salt-washed colors and mismatched furniture gave off a nostalgic vibe, yet the tiny shop was thoroughly modern and oh, so cozy.

After a few years, new opportunities presented themselves and Eric moved Southern Bean Coffee Shop to the Dunes Shops, at the intersection of the Bypass and White Street in Kitty Hawk. The location was immediately embraced by new neighbors, and the regulars drove the extra two miles south to get their favorite coffee.

Just a few blocks away from the new shop is the beach where Gardner mentored many young surfers, as well as employees. In January 2013, Gardner died suddenly at age forty-seven, and a memorial was erected in his memory in the sand dune at the end of White Street.

Happy Wrap

1 large specialty tortilla shell smeared with peanut butter, plain yogurt and honey, topped with banana and crunchy-sweet granola.

STATION SIX

Kitty Hawk

Station Six restaurant owner and operator Mary Marvel "Mimi" Adams could be a little intimidating for some employees. She demanded perfection and had little tolerance for anything other than her ultra-high standards of service.

It didn't take long to know if the gig was right or not for you. Said Laura Cloyes Deel, "Mimi was terrifying!"

"It was my first kitchen job ever so I was completely clueless and I was the only girl!" Laughing, she added, "Then, I got to know her. It was a great job—she taught me so much."

In 1985, Mimi bought the original Kitty Hawk Beach Lifesaving Station and transformed it into Station Six Restaurant, an upscale eatery with a certain flair. This was dignified dining. This wasn't a just-fancy-enough-for-the-vacation-folk kind of place. When you walked in, you could almost smell that children were not really welcome. The aromas were incredibly adult,

Above: Local businesswoman Mimi Adams, owner and operator of Station Six in Kitty Hawk, was known for letting her staff know exactly what was expected of them, their very best and then some. *Photo by Drew C. Wilson, courtesy Outer Banks History Center.*

Right: Expectations were high, and polishing wine glasses pre-service ensured that servers had sparkling stemware when presenting and opening high-dollar bottles of wine. *Photo by Drew C. Wilson, courtesy Outer Banks History Center.*

sophisticated, European: fresh seafood, top butchery cuts, aperitifs and ports. Deel continued:

> *I learned much of what I know about a professional kitchen in the kitchen at Station Six, from her, Robert Farmer and others. Food safety, color coded cutting boards, kitchen lingo such as "behind! Hot pan! 86, heard!" How to garnish a plate, how to put together meal components so as not to have a beige plate ever! Robert Brenner taught me all about cleanliness in a professional kitchen and how to get really prepared before doing any breaking down and cleaning.*

Mimi first ventured to the Outer Banks in 1964, buying property shortly thereafter, and made it her home permanently in 1980. She and her husband, Frank, practiced real estate before opening the first eatery in Duck, the Duck Deli, a casual sandwich shop.

Lou Boender Bartscher, owner of Carolina Moon Gallery, remembered, "I loved Station Six. I would hit the bar with Greg Bennett on the way from our stores in Duck. Sometimes the wind would be blowing so hard it would be difficult to open the front door. Determination would take over and in I would be to enjoy champagne after a hard day of work. Oh, yeah, the food was good."

The reputation of the restaurant was sterling, and Swiss chef Beat Zuttel led the kitchen team for a time and added his upscale spin to the meals served at Station Six. His recipe calls for fresh tiger shark, but firm fish may be substituted.

Coujons of Tiger Shark "Huron"
Chef Beat Zuttel
Serves 4

2 pounds tiger shark, cut in strips
1 lime, juiced
5 teaspoons chopped garlic
Dash white Worcestershire sauce
1 tablespoon flour
1 tablespoon julienned fresh ginger
2 tablespoons julienned zucchini
2 tablespoons julienned carrots

2 tablespoons julienned squash
2 tablespoons julienned tomatoes
4 ounces safflower oil
12 ounces cooked long grain rice

Marinate the shark in lime, garlic and Worcestershire for 1 minute. Then dip into the flour. Sauté the shark in hot oil, add the julienned vegetables to the fish and sauté until done. Serve in rice ring.

ALICE'S AT SEA RANCH
Kill Devil Hills

"There is a new Sea Ranch and this is it!" exclaimed Isabel G. Murphy in her popular guide book *Dining on the Outer Banks*, published in 1964. According to the guide, the first Sea Ranch was located at the entrance of Southern Shores, on the oceanfront. Murphy shared that the owner and operator, Alice Sykes, "fought mother nature as long as she could stand and moved her operations south, to the current location, in Kill Devil Hills."

Go ask Alice had a special meaning to clientele of a certain distinction at this seaside eatery inside the Sea Ranch Hotel in Kill Devil Hills. Alice Sykes was the feisty and popular owner of the oceanfront hotel and restaurant, and many say she was a bit of a matchmaker. Rumors, or perhaps legends, abound about her ability to help gentlemen procure dates. It might all just have been wishful thinking and gum flapping, others say.

"Not true," wrote her grandson Cliff Blakely on a Facebook thread,

> *Alice Sykes always believed that a little booze and "implied sex" would make you money. Sexy was all she ever wanted the Ranch to be. At either the Southern Shores or the KDH locations. For a time some girls tried to run an escort service out of the lounge. When Alice got wind of it, she shut them down. She also believed that what a guest did in their hotel room was their own business.*

"I worked there in the 80s," shared Patricia B. Jenkins. "I remember cleaning the owners room. That sucker was so fancy, all pink and frilly, and her and those eye covers that you put over your eyes while sleeping," she laughed. "I have no idea what you call them, but I sure thought she was, like a queen or something. I was young and had never met anyone like her before!"

"I wore evening gowns as a desk clerk," remembered Marianna Funk.

It was the place to be if you were on the social circuit, the political circuit or the party circuit. No matter your people, Alice welcomed all with reserved sparkle. She was no pushover, and if she didn't care for you, well, she had a hard time hiding it.

That she was a pioneer in the tourism and hospitality business in Dare County is rarely disputed. She built the original Sea Ranch in 1952 in Southern Shores. As this first location was taken by the Ash Wednesday Storm, Alice built the new Sea Ranch in Kill Devil Hills in 1962 where it stands today.

Isabel Murphy went into further detail:

> *The Sea Ranch dining room is glass-walled from floor to ceiling, and from any table in this Seascape Room, diners have a view of the ocean beach, swimming pool patio and surrounding scenery. On the landward side, the beautiful Wright Memorial Monument atop Big Kill Devil Hill, towers over the area reminding one that on this spot the famous Wright brothers made their history-making first flight.*

She also was a big fan of the menu:

> *They serve the most delicious seafood casserole here I've ever eaten. It's a combination of lobster, crabmeat, shrimp, and other ocean dainties, and has that certain something that is hard to define, but SO good. And who can resist when such things as Wanchese Crab with Lillie's special sauce, shows up on the menu; and the palate-pleasing Blue Fish Amandine, Smithfield Ham with Imperial Crab; Shrimp De Jonghe; Prime Ribs of Beef, steaks broiled to perfection, and dozens of other gourmet delights for your choosing.*

Murphy was not just a fan, she was kind of starry-eyed about this restaurant, and for such fashionable reasons. Her advertorial waxed poetic about local vegetables and how eating them may or may not be good for the feminine physique,

> *As for the Sea Ranch vegetables, they're famous! Gathered fresh daily from Currituck farms and gardens in the early morning while still wet with*

The Sea Ranch dining room when owned and operated by Alice Sykes. *Photo by Chas. D'Amours, courtesy Outer Banks History Center.*

dew, they're cooked just right and served hot to your table while you dine, and there's seconds too. If fried okra is your dish, you will get it there, also French fried eggplant, string beans with country ham, squash au gratin, scalloped cabbage, all this and more, at the Sea Ranch. All of this is a sure diet-breaker and if you're trying to keep that girlish figure, forget it, but who cares about curves when they throw you one like this. So let yourself go and eat away, it all makes for a feeling of well-being, and a happy vacation too.

It was a different time; ABC permits hadn't come in to play yet, and brown bagging was the way to drink. The bars provided setups, usually a glass with ice and a mixer, like cola or soda water.

Liquor by the drink wasn't available in Kill Devil Hills or Nags Head until 1980. Kitty Hawk didn't allow it until in 1982 and Duck in 1986.

Said Richard Holder, "It was cool seeing folks get dressed up for dinner and stop by their locker to pick up their booze for dinner."

Above: The Sea Ranch hotel has been updated many times over the years, including the sign. Windy conditions make it necessary. *Photo by the author.*

Below: The Sea Ranch hotel, in Kill Devil Hills, has maintained an oceanside restaurant since Alice Sykes was the owner. This outdoor patio setting, now called Beachside Bistro, is bordered by dunes and sea oats with the ocean just a few yards away. *Photo by the author.*

As for music, Blakely added, "Back, back in the day it was Dick Bessette. Starting in the early 80s, it was his son Buzz Bessette, [who] played for us for almost 17 years. The liquor lockers were painted a dark blue, but, I covered them with a pinkish carpet after we got liquor by the drink."

Post-Alice eateries that have made their home in the still-operating hotel include Third Street Oceanfront Grill and Dining Room, Oceanfront Trellis, the Pearl and, currently, Beachside Bistro. None was quite like Alice's place.

Alice Sykes's Crab Bisque

½ pound butter
2 tablespoons flour
2 cups milk
1 teaspoon salt
¼ teaspoon red pepper
¼ teaspoon mace
¼ teaspoon nutmeg
1 pound fresh back fin crab meat
3 cups thin coffee cream
Sherry, to taste

Melt butter in top of double boiler. Add flour and blend. Add milk and cook, stirring until thickened. Add seasonings and crab. When ready to serve, add cream and heat. Place one bouillon spoon of sherry in a bouillon cup, add bisque and serve.

Sea Ranch Crab Cakes

1 teaspoon salt
1 tablespoon Accent
½ teaspoons pepper
2 tablespoon Worcestershire sauce
1 teaspoon Tabasco
2 eggs, beaten
¼ cup mustard
½ cup mayonnaise
1 cup cracker meal

1 pound back fin crab meat
Cracker meal, for breading

Mix first 9 ingredients well; add crab meat and mix with hands. Make into small balls and roll in cracker meal. Press into patties and again roll in cracker meal. Deep fry at 350 degrees until brown. Serve with lemon and tartar sauce.

CROATAN INN, PAPAGAYO'S, QUAGMIRES

Kill Devil Hills

Croatan Inn, a seaside hotel with dining and a legendary menu, was built in the 1930s by Skipper and Bernie Griggs, just after Virginia Dare Trail was paved. Skipper Griggs also was the owner of the visiting sportsmen's favorite, the Hampton Lodge, in the Waterlily village of Currituck County. She had a direct line to clientele, and it was not hard to convince them to return to the oceanfront to vacation with their families.

In 1964, in *Dining on the Outer Banks*, Isabel Murphy wrote,

> *In the culinary department, the Croatan kitchen has been undergoing re-organization since last summer, with new and up-to-date equipment installed in readiness for the summer season. Tom Briggs is the big boss of the food department and it is under his watchful eye that meals are kept up to standard. With their new kitchen all set to go, Tom and Susie are planning for the most enjoyable meals ever at the Croatan.*
>
> *Their broiled steaks are all best western meats, and the fried chicken, lobster tails stuffed with crabmeat, soft shell crabs, broiled shrimp in lemon butter, as well as the broiled bluefish, are really very special. There is a different seafood special every day, and you will enjoy the shrimp and crabmeat salad, and for a real treat try their clam chowder. Home-made rolls, corn muffins, fresh vegetables and home-made pies, make Croatan meals a delight.*
>
> *The Croatan's oceanside picture-windowed dining room is spacious and cool, and the red and white striped awning decor is especially attractive. The Wheel House with its sea-going atmosphere and adjoining sundeck overlooking the ocean and beach, is a favorite spot with guests.*

Advertisement for Croatan Inn as printed in *Surfside News*, 1977. *From the private collection of Melody Leckie.*

According to author and local historian Sarah Downing, many of the families who vacationed at the inn year after year were attracted to its casual beach atmosphere and home-cooked food. Records show that Tom and Susie Briggs later took over ownership. In the 1960s, the Briggses added the Motor Lodge to the original building. The property was then owned by Robert and Laura Tupper.

James's Deviled Clams
Croatan Inn Dining Room

4 teaspoons butter
1 small onion, minced
4 tablespoons flour
¼ teaspoon dry mustard
¾ cup milk
1 egg yolk, slightly beaten

½ cup soft bread crumbs
1 teaspoon chopped parsley
1 pint clams, chopped

Melt butter, add onion, cook until soft. Add flour and mustard, stirring until smooth. Add milk and cook until thick. Remove mixture from heat and stir in egg yolk, crumbs, parsley and seasonings. Place chopped clams in a saucepan and heat through. Drain clams of most liquid, and combine with sauce. Mixture should be soft, but not runny. Heap into clam shells. Top with bread crumbs. Crumbs may be mixed with grated cheese. Place under broiler until crumbs are toasted.

Croatan Inn Shrimp Creole

½ cup chopped onion
½ cup chopped celery
1 clove garlic, minced
3 tablespoons salad oil
1 can or 2 cups diced tomatoes
½ can or 1 cup tomato sauce
½ teaspoon salt
1 teaspoon sugar
½ to 1 teaspoon chili powder
1 tablespoon Worcestershire sauce
1 teaspoon cornstarch
2 teaspoons cold water
1 ½ pounds shrimp
½ cup chopped green peppers

Cook onion, celery and garlic in hot oil until tender. Add tomatoes, tomato sauce and seasonings. Simmer uncovered for 45 minutes. Mix cornstarch and water, stir in sauce, cook until mixture thickens. Add shelled shrimp and green peppers, cover, simmer until shrimp and peppers are done, about 5 minutes/ A dash of Tabasco can be added before creole is served. Serve over rice.

One of the most iconic photos of the '80s was this photo of Papagayo's server Lisa Ling Fike balancing her tray for the photographer, for just long enough, though, the food was hot and it had to get to the table. *Photo by Drew C. Wilson, courtesy Outer Banks History Center.*

A postcard published by the Collins Co. shows the cozy atmosphere of the Croatan Inn. The card advertised, "On the ocean front. Club like atmosphere. Dining room terrace, sun deck for the social hour." *From the private collection of Melody Leckie.*

Advertisement for Papagayo from *Surfside News*, 1982. *From private collection of Melody Leckie.*

In a 2006 article for the *Virginian-Pilot*, Kristin Davis wrote, "Rick Suberman later bought the old hotel and opened Papagayos, a popular Mexican and seafood restaurant." That was in 1981.

Davis went on to quote longtime resident Billy Moseley, who said, "In the early '80s, anybody that was anybody was here on the ocean deck. I remember sitting up there on the deck with a pitcher of margaritas and seafood and spinach enchiladas."

Known as a locals' hangout, the back deck, facing the ocean, was especially popular on Sundays. The team had a long and successful run and closed in 1995.

Papagayo's Crab Enchiladas

Sherri Ward Lingg shared the recipe for these crab enchiladas on social media; she says that you can substitute chicken for the crab.

½ onion, finely chopped
Butter
1 teaspoon minced garlic
2 cups lump crab meat
1 cup cream cheese, softened and whipped
Salt and white pepper, to taste
Corn tortillas
Mexican cheese, grated

Sauce

1 cup whipping cream
¼ cup sour cream
1 tablespoon cornstarch
1 tablespoon cold water
Salt and white pepper, to taste

Sauté onion in butter with minced garlic. Add crab* and cream cheese and salt and white pepper to taste.

In a sauce pan, bring to boil whipping cream and sour cream. Then whisk in cornstarch mixed with cold water. Salt and white pepper to taste.

Fry corn tortillas in oil for 5–6 seconds and fill with crab mixture. Roll and put into greased baking dish. Pour sauce over and top with Mexican cheese blend. Bake at 400 degrees until bubbly.
*Can use chicken

Papagayo's Enchiladas Verde
Nora Spaeth shared this recipe.

1 cup plus 2 tablespoons minced onion
3 tablespoons oil
8 ounces cream cheese
1 ⅔ cups milk
2 pounds chicken
1 ½ teaspoons salt
½ teaspoon white pepper
Corn or flour tortillas
1 tablespoon flour
1 sixteen-ounce jar green taco sauce
1 can chopped green chilies

Sauté 1 cup onion in 2 tablespoons oil. Add cream cheese and ⅔ cup milk. Whisk over medium heat until smooth. Remove from heat. Add chicken, 1 teaspoon salt and white pepper. Let cool in refrigerator. When cool, roll filling inside tortillas. Corn tortillas roll better if they are quickly fried, just seconds, in a bit of hot oil. Place filled tortillas, seam side down, in a greased baking dish.

Sauté 2 tablespoons onion in 1 tablespoon oil until soft. Add flour and whisk briefly. Add 1 cup milk. Bring to a boil and continue to whisk. Add ½ teaspoon salt, taco sauce and green chilies. Simmer 5 minutes and pour over enchiladas. Bake until heated through.

In 1996, John Kirchmier bought the property from Suberman. John and his brother, Charles Kirchmier, and their partner, Judy Fisher, renovated the restaurant, changed the name to Quagmires on the Beach, and ran it until 2003. Quagmires served similar enchiladas and plenty of margaritas, but with a bit of a different vibe.

The building was demolished in 2006, and the property is now home to a condo unit complex called Croatan Inn Surf Club.

THE PIT

Nags Head/Kill Devil Hills

In the eighties, dinner and a show usually meant casual eating, followed by some form of pogo-hop-slam-moshing to a band with a semi-provocative name.

In a small shack-like structure next to Tortuga's, on the Beach Road in Nags Head, Ben Sproul and Steve Paul presented the Outer Banks with the Pit. Skateboarding, music, surfing and sustaining on cheap, quality food was the vibe. Well, that and drinking a lot of beer. The cheap food was a vibe; the guys didn't sell much food until they moved to Kill Devil Hills and added a kitchen.

Said Sproul,

> *When we opened on the beach road in 1994, we did not actually serve any food, just Hostess Hohos and Gatorade. Back then, we made a name for ourselves by having free concerts outside on a flatbed trailer to kick off the summer. We were in our late 20s and had personal relationships with a whole bunch of the touring bands at the time. They would stay at our houses when they played at other venues, too.*

The sign on the original building said "boards—grub—cloth." The guys sold boards and fashion and hipness, and their tribe responded. The Pit was as much a place to be as a place to shop or listen to music or pick up skate tips, though all that happened, too.

By the 2010s, everything had changed; the original clients were now parents of teens, and the vibe had definitely changed. The partners moved out of the original location in 1996 and into a vintage log cabin on the bypass. In the spring of 2000, they raised the cabin to its present height to create a venue space below.

They sweated the details, too. Design-centric, the men scrutinized every inch of the buildings' design on the new property. There is parking under one of the two-part buildings, one that is still operated as three-thousand-square-foot retail space called the Pit Surf Shop.

In the new space, the Pit served food, beer and a tiny bit of wine and introduced many an obscure band. It also brought in some bigger name acts and hosted teen nights. To stay in business on the Outer Banks demands relevancy. Teens hung out, as they have always hung out, in a chaperoned, hip environment with food and bands, just no beer. It worked.

Overstuffed burritos were a house specialty at the Pit. The multileveled club gave the impression of a house party; the construction was a nod to the old-school Nags Head style of architecture. The restaurant in the new property was called Boardriders' Grill. *Photo by Ben Sproul.*

The Pit was a local hangout that grew from a beach road shack to a two buildings with a kitchen industry. Underground parking and owner artwork were a few of the details added as the business at the Pit Surf Shop and Boardriders' Grill grew. *Photo by Ben Sproul.*

Music remained a big deal for the business, "A high point may have been landing a date on The Misfits 25th Anniversary Tour in 2002," Sproul enthused.

> *By far the smallest room they ever played that year, most of their giant skull stage set pieces wouldn't fit through the door, much less on our modest stage. The roadies were flummoxed (and that is putting it nicely), but in the end it was an epic show by titans of our generation, inspired to accept our tiny $7,500 offer (way below their going rate), based of our reputation for taking such good care of other legends of punk, like Murphy's Law and Clutch, who also generally played much much larger venues.*
>
> *We never actually even said "surf shop" on our first sign. We thought we were being cool and hip. But I am sure we were confused and lots of people! The first sign at the bypass location in '96 rebranded The Pit as a "Surf Hangout." That moniker lasted until '99, with the hurricane blew the sign down. The next sign graduated to Bar and Grill. Eventually, I rebranded the restaurant and nightclub portion as The Boardriders Grill.*

The owners sold the shop in 2012 and the restaurant and club portion of the business a few years ago to the Booty Treat folks to carry on new traditions.

PORT O'CALL

Kill Devil Hills

Frank Gajar was a multitasking entrepreneur with a quirky vision. Owner, operator and head designer of the Port O'Call Restaurant and Gas Light Saloon in Kill Devil Hills, Gajar brought "Victorian Western" to the Outer Banks.

His characteristic swagger and lit cigarette stance belied his devotion to art and aesthetics. When he added on to his restaurant, his art collection and gallery were what really grew. Of course, everything was for sale. Everything. Make him an offer.

Gajar purchased the property in 1977, when he was just thirty-five years old. The business was originally built and called Port O'Call Restaurant by owners Nancy Aycock and Neil Loy, but Gajar slightly modified the name

Port O'Call Restaurant in Kill Devil Hills was known for lavish displays of fare. Pictured here are owner Frank Gajar and one of his chefs in 1979. *Courtesy of Stephanie Gajar.*

to fit his theme. He also began modifying the building. He knew from the beginning that wrought iron and vintage lighting elements and one-of-a-kind art would create the elegant ambiance he sought.

An unexpected choice for a restaurateur, Gajar held advanced degrees in economics from Cornell and the University of North Carolina. He had also worked in finance for the Hotel Roanoke in Virginia, where he fell in love with the luxurious colonial era aesthetic. Oh, and he also served in the U.S Army from 1962 to 1967 as a helicopter pilot and artillery officer with tours of duty in Frankfurt, West Germany, and Vietnam. He was honorably discharged with the rank of captain and received the Vietnam Service Medal, the National Defense Service Medal and the Air Medal with Oak Leaf Cluster.

Former employee Frank Tansky shared,

> *As his bar manager, he was more of a mentor to me over a 30-year period, I would call him for advice or to chat regularly no matter where I was living at the time. I worked for him from the late 80s, again for a stretch*

Port O'Call Restaurant before expansions. *Photo by Roger Meekins, courtesy Outer Banks History Center.*

in the late 90s and came back as a favor to him in 2011 (he made it extremely lucrative, enough for me to put my business on hold for a summer season). Our late nights early mornings reconciling the till often included very meaningful intercourse that I still draw upon for decision making to this day.

Frank was know for his crankiness towards some employees, but in my experience, he was an absolute joy to work for. If you knew what you were doing, made a sincere effort, and had a strong work ethic, having Frank Gajar in your corner was priceless and for me turned into a lifelong friendship. Personally, he was by far the best boss I EVER had. Every year I visited the OBX, I would spend literally a couple hours in his cramped office catching up and shooting the breeze while inhaling about a cigarette pack's worth of second hand smoke.

Gajar loved that restaurant like a child and was second to none when when interacting with his customers. Like many OBX restaurateurs, he had an almost cult-like following. In addition to the passion for his restaurant was his ability to acquire unique items and stunning jewelry for his gift *shop. One could see the twinkle in Frank's eye appear once he was standing behind one of his many showcases. Gajar's eye for unique and desirable wares was impressive. Frank was truly in his element when when the conversation turned to items for sale in the restaurant. From knickknacks, fine art and the beautiful diamond jewelry in a showcase customers had to walk by to enter the dining room, to the incredible wall sconces and chandeliers used to illuminate the dining room, I don't think there was anything in that entire building he would not have sold for a profit. Gajar's business and deal making savvy was an impressive thing to witness first hand.*

Frank was not easily distracted and when his attention was upon a customer, be it restaurant or gift shop, he had a way of making people feel as if there was nothing more important than that person, in that moment, and their questions or concerns. For some 3 decades I always asked "Frank, you probably have more money than you could spend in another entire lifetime. When or why don't you retire?" His response never changed in 30 years. He would chuckle and say in his deep baritone voice, "Tansky, they are going to carry me out of here on a stretcher." Sadly enough Frank Gajar passed away a couple years ago, working right up until the day he died.

Gajar was indeed an amicable host, and his friend and longtime maitre d' Ferdinand Phipps of Jamaica kept the pace and gave the place an over-the-top worldly charm. It wasn't just his accent either—Phipps taught restaurant etiquette to a ragtag group of wait staff year after year after year by gently chiding and cuffing. They both were fond of nicknaming. Phipps called me the Silver Fox—oh, I can hear him—and Gajar called me the Child Bride. My hair was bleached to blue-white at the time I worked with Phipps, and my later marriages inspired the other.

Former bartender Chris Muniec remembered:

Mr. Phipps worked for one of the big super luxury hotel chains in the middle of the 20th century and he and his team would travel around the world opening new restaurants and training the staff to serve in the manner of that Hotel chain. He brought all of that wonderful, modern, French American service to the Port O' Call. I heard stories of his flaming coffees where they would peel the orange into a long, string rind at the table and run Brandy down that spiraled fruit and light it on fire, as it set the coffee on fire. They also offered tableside service for Caesar salad and various sautés, it was pretty classic and classy.

Waiter Dermot Doyne (*left*) and maitre d' Ferdinand Phipps during dinner service at Port O' Call restaurant in Kill Devil Hills, in the mid-1980s. *Courtesy of Dermot Doyne.*

The Port O'Call Restaurant hosted many charity events. This one was for the Dare County Arts Council and shows an example of his décor. *Photo by the author.*

Phipps, as he was called by Frank, who called Frank, Frank, was a customer favorite. People loved him. People loved Gajar, too. Just in a different way.

Frank was known to be a bit frugal. While his skill in repairing his own equipment was commendable, there are many more stories like this one from Muniec:

> *An early story that I was told but did not live through his when Frank took over the restaurant it had the most ugly curtains imaginable and the waiters suffered under those curtains till one day they came down and new curtains went up and everyone rejoiced only to find out that Miss Margaret (his lady friend at the time) had taken the old fabric and sewed them into vests for the waiters to wear at service. So, the ghost of hated curtains returned to haunt the staff.*

Known for an extensive menu that included everything from crab bisque to prime rib to crab de jonghe, the restaurant somehow managed to pull off a slightly casual yet still elegant dining atmosphere, even when there was a mini rock-and-roll bar in the next room.

Muniec noted that "every restaurant nowadays is offering additional items for sale [but] Frank once told me that he was the first to have a gift shop attached to his restaurant and I can remember nights around Christmas when we might have done two or three tables and then sold

Captain Frank Gajar, owner of Port O'Call Restaurant. *Courtesy of Stephanie Gajar.*

70

$2,000 worth of jewelry to returning fisherman who had cash in their pockets and no Christmas for sweetie."

In an article by Michelle Wagner in the *Outer Banks Sentinel*, Gajar's daughter, Stephanie Gajar, said, "He was reluctant to get into rock 'n roll, but when he realized how much money he could make, he decided the broken chairs were worth it. My dad wasn't a rock 'n roll guy." Stephanie worked at the Port O' Call during a few summers and helped with a number of his projects over the years.

"He was there at the restaurant almost nonstop for forty years and was very reluctant to go on vacation and leave it," she said of her father. "That was his life...I like to think his spirit is still there."

BRIDGES SEAFOOD

Colington

When the reason you had a restaurant was to highlight the soft-shell blue crab operation next door, you know there were some pretty phenomenal crab dishes on the menu at Bridges Seafood just over the first bridge onto Little Colington Island.

Nestled up next to a mosquito ditch, really, a slash in Colington Creek, the house next door to the restaurant packed out startling amounts of soft-shell crabs. The crabs were brought in by boat, directly to the crab house, which looked suspiciously like a brick ranch-style home from the road. Many are still surprised to learn that in 2019, Murray Bridges, his wife and his daughter, Kissy, still pack soft-shell crabs today and fill as many as six tractor trailer trucks worth of crabs to ship north every day in season.

Colington Soft-Shell Crabs with Ginger Sauce

4 large soft-shell crabs, mustard removed
Flour
4 tablespoons peanut oil
3 tablespoons onion, finely minced
2 tablespoons finely minced fresh ginger root
¼ cup chicken stock

1 tablespoon soy sauce
2 tablespoons dry sherry
2 teaspoons cornstarch
Fresh scallions for garnish

Coat soft-shells with flour. Heat a sauté pan over medium high heat until hot. Add 2 tablespoons peanut oil and swirl around pan. Sauté soft-shells and remove just before they are done. Add the remainder of the oil to the pan; add onion and ginger and sauté 1 minute. Add stock, soy sauce and sherry and bring to a boil. Add cornstarch and thicken. Add soft-shells and coat with sauce. Serve with white rice. Garnish with fresh scallions.

How to Clean a Soft-Shell Crab

When you are ready to cook soft-shell crabs, bring them home alive for the ultimate softie experience. Cleaning them is easy and fairly quick once you practice a time or two.

1. Hold crab in one hand, belly side down, and with the other hand, snip off the front of the shell, just behind the eyes, in a quick, clean, cut. You can use scissors or place the crab on a cutting board and use a sturdy, sharp knife.
2. Lift each side of the back shell and remove the gills, sometimes called deadmen.
3. Turn the crab over and remove the hinged part of the shell, called the apron.
4. Tomalley or not tomalley? Uniquely flavored, most people either love or hate the mustard-colored liver and pancreas. If you do not wish to keep the tomalley, now is the time to remove it. Give the crab a gentle but firm squeeze to expel the innards. You might need to use your fingers to get it all.
5. When crabs are cleaned and waiting to be cooked, place them on their backs so the back shell remains moist.
6. Use immediately.

Kissy Bridges packs soft-shell crabs at her family business, Endurance Seafood, in Colington. *Photo by the author.*

Sautéed, also called pan-fried, soft-shell blue crabs, are a beloved specialty on Outer Banks menus. *Photo by the author.*

OUTER BANKS EPICUREAN

Colington

Yes, I have my own lost restaurant. Sometimes, though, it is tempting for me to think about Outer Banks Epicurean as an eighteen-month pop-up. The plan was to make it much longer, but Hurricane Irene helped change the trajectory.

In addition to offering heat-and-eat meals, I offered cooking classes, demonstrations and food-based tours. I had a soft-shell crab tour: in season, we would walk across the street to Endurance Seafood, see the crab shedders, learn why the light shines so bright for twenty-four hours a day, see a crab molt, wow!, then walk back to the kitchen across the street to cook some soft-shells.

The building was plumbed to handle sea water for making sea salt, my other business, Outer Banks SeaSalt. I had a one-thousand-gallon tank installed behind the building; it held ocean water, and a pump connected to pipes under the building pushed it to a faucet in the commercial kitchen. I could place a pot under the faucet, and when I turned it on, sea water would come out—it was pretty fabulous, for as long as it lasted. Hurricane Irene did the most damage to this system and rendered it useless.

Outer Banks Epicurean limped along for a few months after the hurricane but closed officially in October 2011. The catering business survived for a few more years until focus switched to just making SeaSalt, well, and writing.

I am sharing a few of my most requested recipes. Two of the most popular items on my catering menu were Tuna Ceviche and Jumbo Lump Crab Grilled Cheese Squares. They are crowd pleasers and easy to make and assemble just as guests arrive.

The seafood lasagna is best made with fresh Outer Banks seafood. Use what you can, where you are; U.S. wild-caught is always the best option. Same for the shrimp in the shrimp and grits. Please do not use imported shrimp. There is no substitute for soft-shell crabs. Oh, you can use the recipe with other seafood, but it will not be the same, not even close. You must buy the crabs live or use them the same day you have your fishmonger clean them.

The cupcakes are from Rose Levy Beranbaum's book *The Cake Bible*, but the frosting is pure childhood fantasy, piped right on top.

Tuna Ceviche

2 pounds yellowfin tuna, cut into bite-sized pieces
Juice of 4 limes plus juice of 3 lemons
Handful cilantro, chopped
¼ cup minced sweet onion
¼ cup fresh minced jalapeño pepper (more or less, added to taste)
Sea salt
Cracked pepper

Combine all ingredients and chill at least 4 hours before serving. Plate on a mix of local salad greens and a handful of blue corn chips. Yields 6 portions.

Shrimp and Grits with Red-Eye Gravy

¼ pound country ham, cut into half-inch pieces
2 pounds peeled and deveined local shrimp
¼ stick plus 2 tablespoons unsalted butter
2 tablespoons unbleached all-purpose flour
2 cups fresh, strong coffee
¼ cup heavy cream
Sea salt and cracked black pepper

In a large cast-iron skillet, cook the country ham for 2–3 minutes over medium–high heat. You will not need to add anything to the pan before you add the ham if you have a well-seasoned pan. Some of the ham will stick to the bottom of the pan. These yummy bits are called fond and will be the base of your gravy. Next, add your shrimp. Move them around in the pan as they cook. The water content of the shrimp will help them not stick to the pan. The shrimp will start to brown and caramelize, and the flavors of the shrimp and ham will have a chance to marry before the rest of the ingredients arrive.

When the shrimp are almost cooked, remove the duo from the pan. Return the pan to the stovetop, add 2 teaspoons of butter and melt on medium heat. Sprinkle in your flour and immediately whisk the butter and flour and watch it closely. You will want to stir often and cook just until the raw taste of flour becomes nutty and sweet. At that point, add your coffee and continue to whisk. Keep whisking and you may not have a lumpy gravy. While still moving the sauce around in the pan, add the heavy cream. If your heat is too high, you may absorb the liquid too fast. If that happens, you can always add more coffee, so make sure you have a bit extra on hand.

At this point, you can add sea salt and pepper to taste and the rest of the butter. Remove from heat when you add the butter and stir continuously until butter is incorporated and you have a smooth, elegant sauce.

If you have a few lumps and they are not bits of country ham, you may want to strain the gravy. All you need to do is pass the gravy through a fine strainer over a bowl then return the gravy to a clean saucepan.

Add the shrimp and ham to the pan gravy and warm until the shrimp finish cooking. Try not to overcook the shrimp. They like to curl into themselves loosely to let you know they are ready. Serve immediately over stone ground grits.

Shrimp and country ham in a cast-iron skillet, for shrimp and grits with red-eye gravy. *Photo by the author.*

Stone Ground Grits

3 cups water
Sea salt and pepper
1 cup milk
1 cup stone ground grits—NOT instant grits

Place water and milk in a heavy saucepan with a dash of sea salt and heat to simmer. Stir in grits and stir some more. Grits will start to thicken, and large bubbles will rise to the surface. When this happens, cover and reduce the heat to very low, and continue to simmer for about 5 minutes then turn off the heat, cover and do not touch for 20 minutes. The grits will be very tender. At this point, you could add a bit of cheese, a bunch of butter or just a touch more sea salt and cracked pepper to preference.

Country Ham

Go ahead and do it. Commit to a whole country ham. Take the time to soak it and then slow cook it and carve it. The instructions come on the bag. It is easy, and you have country ham to put in the freezer. Imagine the possibilities, all year long, really. It is a lot of ham, but you do save money per pound and your meat isn't soaked in sodium solutions like most county ham slices you find in the grocery stores. Cook your ham a few days before you need it.

Jumbo Lump Crab Grilled Cheese Squares

1 pound cream cheese
1 pound sharp cheddar, shredded
2 green onions, chopped
1 pound local jumbo lump blue crab
Dash of Tabasco sauce
16 slices your favorite real bread
1 stick of butter for grilling sandwiches

Blue crab grilled cheese sandwiches, perfect for party bites, were an Epicurean catering favorite. *Photo by the author.*

Combine first 5 ingredients and use this mixture as a sandwich fill. Using 2 pieces of bread for each, make 8 sandwiches. Use 1 tablespoon of butter per sandwich to grill in the pan. Secret trick: if in a hurry, put the sandwich in the microwave for 30 seconds to pre-melt the inside of the sandwich. You can now spend less time with it in the pan getting a golden crust while still having it hot on the inside. Presentation: Cut into quarters and offer plenty of napkins. You might want to do this in one big batch in the beginning of the party, let everyone get gooey at once, then put away the pan.

This is a recipe we would make in cooking classes. I taught many classes to multigenerational families in the beautiful oceanfront vacation homes that line our beaches and sounds.

Seafood Lasagna with Tarragon Béchamel

It may seem as if there is a lot to this dish, but it is pretty simple once you read it. You may want to add a few extra minutes for cleanup, though!

1 box lasagna pasta, cooked (homemade pasta is best if you are totally DIY)
1 pound local fish, any type, cut into 1-inch pieces
1 pound steamed local shrimp, peeled, deveined and chopped
1 stick plus 6 tablespoons butter
1 pound local crab meat, jumbo lump
32 ounces ricotta cheese
1 cup chopped green onions
½ gallon milk, whole, organic
¼ cup all-purpose flour
Salt to taste
2 tablespoons dried tarragon
4 cups shredded mozzarella

Start by preparing your parts. You have several components you will need to assemble; all are quite simple, but they do take time. If you have not already, cook your pasta and drain. To save yourself heartache, place each noodle on a piece of parchment paper immediately after draining. Line up several and then top with another piece of parchment until all the pasta is flat and not touching. This isn't a necessary step if you like piecing together the puzzle that happens when the pasta is left to cool in the colander.

Next, cook your fish and shrimp. This is basically a butter baste. Gently warm 6 tablespoons of butter in sauté pan, when foamy, add fish and shrimp. Spoon the butter over and around the seafood until it is completely cooked. I like a mild white fish as well as super fresh tuna. Actually, I haven't met a fish I didn't like in this dish. Spoon seafood into a small bowl and set it aside until time to assemble.

Pick your crab. Pick it again. When your family finds a piece of shell, you can cheerily inform them that they can be guaranteed that the crab is local and hand picked and that shell is proof. You will not find shells in imported, bleached or pre-formed crab nuggets. Try thinking of random crab shells as a local badge of honor.

In medium bowl, combine picked crab meat with ricotta and green onions. Set aside.

Next, make the béchamel sauce. Heat your milk in a saucepan; you will need it warm when you add it to the butter and flour. In a separate, heavy-bottomed saucepan, melt ¼ cup butter and then stir in the flour and cook, stirring constantly, until the paste bubbles. Do not let the roux become brown. This should only take a few minutes. You can tell by taste when you are ready to add the milk. If the roux still tastes like raw flour, cook it a bit longer until it does not. At this point, add the hot milk, a cup at a time, continuing to stir as the sauce thickens. Bring it to a boil. Add salt to taste; lower the heat and cook, stirring for 2 to 3 minutes more. Remove from the heat and stir in dried tarragon. To cool this sauce for later use, cover it with wax paper to prevent a skin from forming. This recipe makes a béchamel that has a little more milk than normal. This will be needed because we are baking with pasta.

In large baking dish, ladle in 2 cups of béchamel sauce to coat the bottom completely. Add a layer of lasagna pasta. Top with half of the crab and ricotta mixture. Top that with half the fish and shrimp and then ladles of the béchamel. Repeat. Top lasagna with all the mozzarella and bake in a 350-degree oven for about 45 minutes or until top cheese is melted and browned. Leftovers freeze nicely.

Fire-Kissed Collards

1 bunch local collards, organic if possible
Good olive oil
2 cloves garlic, minced
Local sea salt

Clean collards by rinsing them under running water in your kitchen sink. Fold each leaf in half and remove the stalk. You can do this with your fingers or with a knife. Leave the leaves folded together. Select 6–8 leaves at a time and roll them up like you were rolling a big cigar or sushi roll. You will then cut the collards like a giant julienne, or like you were cutting a slice off of a roll of sushi. When you are finished, you will have nice long strands of slightly wet greens. Heat an iron skillet until hot and then add a tiny bit of good olive oil. Immediately add the greens and move them around quickly in the pan to wilt. Turn off the heat and add the garlic and sea salt. Continue to move the greens around the pan until they are all wilted. This is a super fast dish. Do not overcook. Feeds 2–4.

Fire-kissed collards, locally grown and quick cooked. *Photo by John Gaw.*

Soft-Shell Blue Crabs with Field Pea Succotash

1 ½ sticks unsalted butter
1 medium local sweet onion, diced
4 ears corn-off-the-cob
3 cups blanched until soft field peas (white acre, pink lady, even lima beans)
2 medium, ripe tomatoes, chopped
Freshly cracked pepper
Sea salt
8 jumbo or whale size soft-shell crabs, cleaned
Unbleached flour for dredging
¼ cup good olive oil
Handful chopped basil leaves

In large cast-iron skillet heat ½ stick of butter until it is frothy. Add onion and cook over medium heat until almost translucent. Add corn, field peas and tomatoes, a generous grind of black pepper and a good size dash of local sea salt. Shake the pan and let it continue to heat over low heat while you cook the soft-shells. Really, this is a quick-cook dish. Do it all at once, no need to cook all day or fret. If the corn is super fresh, you just want a kiss of heat. Remember, you already blanched the field peas.

Next, cook the soft-shells. Start by lightly seasoning both sides of the crabs with a smidge of sea salt and pepper. Lightly dredge the crabs in flour and shake off excess.

Using a heavy-bottomed sauté pan or a cast-iron pan, warm half the olive oil. Increase the heat to high and add ¼ of the remaining butter. When foamy, add dredged soft-shells to the pan. Cook for 3–4 minutes and turn over carefully, watch for popping fat from high water content in crab, reducing the heat to medium. Continue to cook until crab turns from translucent to opaque and has a nice golden exterior. Cook about 2 minutes longer than you think you should. Remove onto platter. Repeat with remaining soft-shells.

Remove pan from heat. Swirl in remaining butter and add a bit of sea salt and fresh basil. Set aside. Place succotash on individual dinner plates, top with two soft-shell crabs and drizzle with basil butter.

Buttermilk Cupcakes

Cake recipe adapted from Rose Levy Beranbaum's The Cake Bible
All ingredients work best at room temperature

4 large egg yolks
⅔ cup buttermilk
1 ½ teaspoons vanilla
2 cups cake flour, sifted
1 cup sugar
1 tablespoon baking powder
½ teaspoon salt
8 tablespoons unsalted butter, softened

Preheat oven to 350. In a medium bowl, gently combine the yolks, about ¼ of the buttermilk and the vanilla. In the bowl of a standing mixer, combine all of the dry ingredients. With the paddle attachment, mix on low for 30 seconds. Add the butter and the remaining buttermilk and continue to mix until everything is moistened. Increase to medium

Right: Country eggs from the Egg Place in Currituck paired with Outer Banks SeaSalt during an Outer Banks Epicurean catering event. *Photo by the author.*

Below: Buttermilk cupcakes with vanilla frosting were one of the best sellers at Outer Banks Epicurean in Colington. *Photo by John Gaw.*

speed (high if you're using a hand mixer) and beat for 1½ minutes. Scrape down the sides of the bowl, then begin gradually adding the egg mixture, which should be done in 3 batches. Beat for 20 seconds between each addition. Scrape down the sides once more.

Pour the batter into paper-lined cupcake pans, 3/5 of the way full. Bake for 20–25 minutes, until a toothpick comes out clean. Let the cupcakes cool for 10 minutes. Then remove from the pan and cool on a rack until room temperature. They can then be frosted, stored in fridge or frozen.

Vanilla Frosting

2 sticks unsalted butter
2 pounds confectioners' sugar
1 cup heavy cream
2 teaspoons real vanilla extract

In a large bowl, cream butter until smooth, then gradually add sugar. Add vanilla to cream and then add that slowly to the sugar and butter. Beat until light and fluffy. If necessary, adjust consistency with more milk or sugar.

MRS. T'S DELI

Nags Head

Even if not what I craved, I had a hard time not ordering the Italian Stallion whenever I ordered from Pauline Tauber, also known as Mrs. T. For whatever reason, the name gave me the giggles—it also tasted great.

Mrs. T was the founder and operator of Mrs. T's Deli in Nags Head. She had many talents, was an empathic, humorous woman and led her family work team with a hard charge and bigger sense of humor.

Mrs. T, as everyone knew her, was born in Cuba. She loved her customers, and her ads shared her philosophy, "Making good things for good people," she was fond of saying.

Pauline Tauber, also known as Mrs. T., and her husband, Moises, stand in their Nags Head deli. *Photo by Drew C. Wilson, courtesy Outer Banks History Center.*

Her shop walls, coolers and cabinets were covered with handwritten 8.5-by-11 paper signs declaring her various sandwich combinations. Each paper held one description; most were horizontal. She had over seventy types of sandwiches; there were a lot of signs. She had grilled subs, chilled subs, sliced meats and cheeses to make your own. She also offered beer and wine with her sandwiches, offering both to consume on-site or to take with you.

Located where Staples is today, the location was easy to access, and she fed a steady stream of people daily. If in a talkative mood, which was mostly, she would share stories of catering for dignitaries in Washington, D.C., including several presidents.

Wrote Catherine Kozak in the *Virginian-Pilot,*

> *When Mrs. T's Deli opened nearly 21 years ago, there was no other eatery on the Outer Banks quite like it. As the establishment shuts its doors for good today, unhappy customers mourn the loss of a one-of-a-kind restaurant that made you feel like you had walked into your favorite aunt's house to enjoy a homemade lunch.*

Located on the corner of a strip mall across from Nags Head Bowling Center, the 1,500-square-foot restaurant once was crammed with quirky cookie jars—all for sale—and souvenirs from Tauber's former restaurant outside Washington, including autographed pictures of a number of presidents.

Always bustling with loyal customers who jockeyed with tourists for a booth in the summer, Mrs. T's was known for its homemade subs, such as the Italian Stallion, and specialties like Outer Banks fries, sprinkled with Old Bay seasoning, and veggie burgers topped with grilled onions.

Before the Taubers moved to the Outer Banks in 1984, the family ran the Capital Plaza Deli in Landover Hills, Maryland, for twenty years. Although part of their service included providing catered lunches to the White House, Mrs. T's daughter, Shirley Tauber, remembered, "The first five years were terrible, with bill collectors and repossessors hounding them."

The family overcame the challenges and built a steady and loyal clientele there as well as on the Outer Banks.

KELLY'S RESTAURANT AND TAVERN

Nags Head

"One night, last week, there were three couples in here for dinner," chuckled Mike Kelly, almost a bit incredulously. "They met here and got married and had kids. They wanted to eat here one last time before we close. Before we made the announcement, I didn't always hear this stuff. Damn, I feel like Cupid!"

Love happened. Food happened. Life happened. So many stories. Thousands and thousands of them. All firmly rooted on a five-acre property in uptown Nags Head.

It is almost easier to compile a list of what did not happen at Kelly's Restaurant and Tavern during the thirty-plus-year lifespan of one of the Outer Banks' most famous eateries than attempt to chronicle what did transpire.

While easy to wax poetic about the nonstop dining, dancing and merrymaking that form the base of infinite memories, it is the hundreds of little love stories and the unbridled benevolence of the owner that have always been the driving force behind the big-number feeding machine, the

Kelly's Restaurant and Tavern, in Kill Devil Hills, pictured here in 2018, waiting for the new owners to tear it down and build a grocery store. *Photo by the author.*

drumming heartbeat that drew people to the dance floor and then kept them coming back.

Since June 18, 1985, the day founder Mike Kelly opened his doors to the public, Kelly's Restaurant and Tavern has employed hundreds of full-time and seasonal workers, hosted dignitaries and ditch diggers with Mike's signature brand of coastal country hospitality and contributed millions to the local economy in the form of tax dollars. Mike also personally funded countless personal emergencies and crises; to help others and his community is deeply inherent in his nature.

Now, it is time for the machine to downshift, just a bit, anyway. Kelly's Restaurant and Tavern closed its doors in early December 2018 and did not reopen for business. Food is still on the agenda for the property; Lidl's grocery store will become the new inhabitant and will build its own glass-fronted shop.

Having had the opportunity to work with owners Mike and wife Willo Kelly in many capacities over the decades, one thing is certain. If they say they will do it, it will get done, and more.

Art auctions, themed fundraisers, drag shows, Easter egg hunts, post–St. Patty Parade hot dogs. Whatever the season, the occasion, the memorial, they shared. No effort was too small for them to lend a hand, cook up some food, donate a gift certificate, burn a tab or share their space for others to also spread a good word and raise funds.

About the Outer Banks landmark, Mike said he looks forward to several milestones as they transition and scale back their businesses, "I want a chance to enjoy them all," he emphasized.

With the closing of the Nags Head location, Mike stressed that the catering operation will not be effected, nor will the operation of Mako's or Pamlico Jack's, both part of Kelly's restaurant group, so, you can still buy those yummy sweet potato and country ham biscuits.

It is hard to imagine that this old friend, stomping grounds for so many, will not be around after the new year. A void has been created in the food and music landscape that will be hard to fill.

"Closing. It's a little bit of everything. Bittersweet for sure, but we are going to make the most of it."

We all will, Mike, we all will. Thanks for the everything.

The padlocked front door at Kelly's Restaurant and Tavern.
Photo by the author.

Sweet Potato Crème Brûlée
By Becky Miller, pastry chef

1 quart heavy cream
4 egg yolks
¾ cup sugar
¾ cup mashed sweet potatoes
1 tablespoon honey
½ teaspoon vanilla
¼ teaspoon cinnamon

Place the cream into a saucepan and cook over medium heat until a light boil. Remove from heat.

In a mixing bowl, whisk together egg yolks and sugar. Add hot cream a little at a time.

In another bowl, mix sweet potatoes, honey, vanilla and cinnamon. Then add in the cream mixture until just combined. Pour the liquid into 8-ounce crème brûlée ramekins (small lip about 3 inches in diameter). Place ramekins in a roasting pan and pour enough hot water into the pan to come halfway up the sides of the ramekins. Bake at 225 for 30 minutes. Cool, then put in refrigerator until ready to serve. When ready to serve, sprinkle sugar on top, and using a torch, melt the sugar to form a crispy top. *Makes approximately 6 (8 ounces).(As printed in Taste of the Beach event program.)*

GANDALF AND COMPANY RESTAURANT AND SEASHORE CAFE

Nags Head

Bob and Jan Kannry had a special kind of magic that drew artists, surfers, rebels, intellects and ingénues, and they all melded together and became one big happy family. Well, something close to that. The stories told confirm that once you joined the staff, you joined the family.

Gandalf's opened in April 1984 and was owned and operated by Bob and Jan Kannry, both of Ohio and longtime Outer Banks residents. They only had a short run; the eatery caught fire in 1987 and the Kannrys were forced to close. The building itself was rehabbed, first in Quagmires and now the present-day Tortuga's Lie.

Janice K. Connors Kannry was a people person and talented cook and so was Bob. He also was the music man. Before moving to the Outer Banks, Bob Kannry created a local acoustic guitar and jazz coffee house in the basement of a local synagogue; on the Outer Banks, he was a jazz DJ on Sunday nights, playing songs from his own record collection.

Genevieve "Genna" Mizzelle Clark shared, "My best memories of Gandalf's are of the stage in the back yard. Just about every local musician played there, most likely for pennies, or for free. I still know and love many of them, although others have passed on. We were family. On my daughter, Maggie's, first birthday...just to show what a family we all were...Bob and Jan shut the restaurant and made it into a private party for Maggie Miles!"

It is appropriate, then, that a former employee, really a family member, shared this recipe—one that commemorates a loving union.

Italian Wedding Soup

In an article in the Beachcomber, *in April 1985, Jan was quoted as saying that this soup is better the day after being made. It is her mom's grandmother's recipe.*

1–2 pounds ground beef
5 eggs
Seasoned bread crumbs
Granulated garlic
Oil for frying
Salt, to taste
6 or more bunches of endive, cleaned and chopped
Chicken broth or chicken base
2 cups diced carrots
2 cups diced onion
3 stalks celery, diced with some tops chopped
4 cups cooked chicken
Parmesan cheese (lots)

Meatballs: In a large bowl, mix ground beef, 2 eggs, seasoned bread crumbs, granulated garlic ('til you can really smell it), black pepper and

1 cup parmesan cheese. Mix well with your hands and form into bite-sized balls. Fry in 3–4 inches of oil until browned; drain on paper towels.

Fill a large pot with water, and with a dash of salt, cook endive until tender, about 1 hour. Drain and put aside. Fill pot with water and add chicken base or broth. Add carrots, celery, onions and bring to a boil. Then add endive, chicken and meatballs; reduce heat and simmer for 45 minutes.

Beat 3 eggs with about ½ cup Parmesan cheese. Bring the soup back to a boil. Pour egg and cheese mix into soup. Take a fork and bring up through the soup.

From Gandalf's private cookbook, anonymously shared.

A RESTAURANT BY GEORGE

Nags Head

Style icon, entrepreneur, visionary, producer, director and star, Norfolk-born restaurateur George Stonewall Crocker Jr. brought elegance, flair, sophistication and design straight onto the sandy runway known at the Outer Banks.

Crocker was a serial entrepreneur who owned the Galleon Esplanade, A Restaurant by George, the Rear View Mirror, the Cabana East Motel, the Beacon Motor Lodge, the Treasure Gallery and the Beach Mart. Crocker was developer of North Ridge, Nags Head Acres, Long Lake and the Enclaves.

He also was a benevolent patron. In 1982, he co-founded the Outer Banks Community Foundation with David Stick, Andy Griffith, Eddie Greene and Ray White.

Local author and publisher Beth Storie reminisced about A Restaurant by George: "For the first few years it was open, after dinner waiters would bring around a box full of long, vibrantly colored cigarettes for the ladies. You'd choose one that matched your outfit and puff away…right there in the restaurant.…It was a different time."

On Facebook, Larry Gray remembered, "An iconic figure on the Outer Banks for many, many years, George Crocker. A visionary in the business world and a leader in the community, he was the founder of the Galleon, built the Beacon Motor Lodge and the Cabana East and help start the Community Foundation. A wonderful person and a real individual."

A Restaurant by George's unique architecture featured a windmill and a party tower. *Photo by Drew C. Wilson, Outer Banks History Center.*

On a Facebook thread, Paige Yoder Celestin reflected, "I had the immense pleasure of working for Mr. Crocker for five summer seasons at A Restaurant by George. A more creative mind and kinder soul never lived. Who remembers 'The Eye of the Needle' and the partying that took place up there!? Ye gads!"

She was referring to the room at the top of the bar with a 360-degree view. The vibe was disco, before, during and after the seventies. At least in that space. Group-sized beverages served in punch bowl vessels with as many straws as needed were popular. Pillows for lounging affirmed the vibe.

Larry Gray agreed: "What a party atmosphere he created and the wonderful individuals who hung out there."

From a 1983 article in the *New York Times* by Gerald Gold:

> *For the big night out, everyone ends up sooner or later at By George's, known officially as A Restaurant, By George. It is a mighty good one. (The owner, George Crocker, also operates one of the most fashionable shops in the area,*

the Galleon.) By George sports a sort of East Indian-African safari decor, rather Maughamish, including wicker fanback chairs, but the cuisine is primarily Continental. There is an exceptionally tasty curry dish, and the ham wrapped in pastry dough is mouth-watering. The prices are generally higher here, but a daily dinner special was only $10.95.

"Sprawling and mazelike, George's in recent years was a favorite place for large community events. Its chalk-white exterior, with gold trim, domes, towers and a windmill, made it one of the region's quirkiest buildings," printed the *Daily Press* in December 2004, not long before the site was demolished.

By George had a good run in the Outer Banks world of food; the original part of the restaurant, which was later the main dining room, was built in the 1960s and operated as a pizza parlor. In 1985, Crocker sold the 13,500-square-foot eatery to Mike Kelly and Frank Gajar, who ran the restaurant as George's Junction Buffet & Saloon until it was demolished in 2004.

French Chocolate Pie
By George S. Crocker

3 egg whites
½ teaspoon salt
1 teaspoon cream of tartar
¾ cup sugar
1 4-ounce can pecans
1 teaspoon vanilla
¼ pound German sweet chocolate
2 tablespoons water
1 tablespoon strong rum
1 pint whipping cream

Combine egg whites, salt and cream of tartar in mixing bowl. Beat until very foamy throughout. Add sugar—2 tablespoons at a time—beating after each addition until sugar is blended. Continue beating until mixture will stand in very stiff peaks. Fold chopped nuts and vanilla in gently.

Spoon into a lightly greased 8-inch pie pan and make a nest-like shell. (Build up around the edges.) Do not allow to go over rim of pan. Bake in slow oven, 300 degrees, for 50 to 55 minutes.

While shell is baking, place chocolate and water in saucepan over low heat. Stir until melted. Cool. Add rum.

Whip cream to soft consistency. Fold chocolate into cooled whipped cream. Pile into shell. Chill at least two hours.

NEWBY'S

Nags Head then Kill Devil Hills

Tim Foard tells great stories. Part of the reason folks liked returning to his sandwich shop was because Tim and his crew were always laughing and joking. If they weren't, it probably meant to be on guard, something was in the works.

"Newby's was my first job on the Outer Banks," Trish Fountain Wilkinson joked on a Facebook thread. "I loved Ken and Tim. They loved to have the new employees water the plastic plants."

"Yep," agreed Ken, "that's classic Tim. He once came to work dressed as a cowboy, complete with chaps and a huge hat. He's also one of the smartest guys I know."

Ken Strayhorn added,

> *The first Newby's was in an old building across from the Drane Cottage, south of Jockey Ridge. The shop was downstairs and upstairs was used as a boarding house for employees. The second shop was custom-built in the winter of 76–77. The original shop was of course in Greenville. I had the pleasure of working in all three shops and even helped build the final shop. The shirts still said "Greenville and Nags Head" because we never got around to updating them.*

Foard explained how Newby's came to be: "Newby's was founded by the late Ed Newbaker on Fifth Street across from ECU and after many years of success, Ed decided to expand the brand. I was fortunate to be part of a great group of Greenville guys and gals that relocated to Nags Head. Years later, my partner and I bought Ed out so that he could pursue his passion and Ed became US water ski champion."

He went on to laugh about hijinks, saying, "In the image you asked about, that is good friend Chip Py who ran a business where, for a fee,

Local entrepreneur Chip Py takes one for the team and waves the company placard on the side of Highway 158, in front of Newby's Sub Shop. *Photo by Drew C. Wilson, Outer Banks History Center.*

he would deliver Gator Grams and Gorilla Grams and Penguin Grams to unsuspecting individuals at their workplace or home or hospital, etc. We had him out front waving that placard to lure patrons."

When I asked him for a recipe, I alluded to one that someone had referenced online. The recipe for the secret sauce. In classic Tim Foard style, he shared the recipe. "The Secret Sauce was made after closing at night with the lights off so that no one could see me strain the seeds out of the leftover juice from a gallon of sliced banana peppers with a bar towel, add salad oil, pinch of salt, pour into squeeze bottles. Just the right amount of greasy heat."

The made-to-order food was available by stepping up to a counter, like a large window into the kitchen. You could eat in or take out. If you ate in, you kinda knew that you would leave sticky bottomed.

Vicki Moulson laughed, "I remember painting the booths before Newby's opened, and we must have mixed the resin wrong because the customers stuck to the booths for half of that first summer."

"That is exactly how it happened," Foard confirmed with his trademark deadpan, "We failed completely."

THE ARLINGTON HOTEL AND DINING ROOM
Nags Head

"Phoebe Hayman has a lifetime [of] experience in food preparation and management," wrote Isabel Murphy in her dining guide, "having been brought up in the hotel business by her parents, the late Captain and Mrs. Nathaniel Gould, who in the early 1900s owned and operated the Roanoke Hotel on Roanoke Island, and later the Tranquil House, which in those days, with electricity, telephones and running water, was far advanced in modern conveniences. The picturesque Tranquil House stood for nearly a century in downtown Manteo until recently demolished to make way for the new Manteo Post Office."

How's that for a whole lot of name dropping? There was more: "In the 1930s the Haymans operated New England House in Manteo, and in 1944 they bought the Arlington Hotel in the area known as Old Nags Head. In 1960 they opened the Seafare which is considered one of the coast's truly fine restaurants. The Arlington, opposite the Seafare, is now operated as a motel in connection with the restaurant."

The Arlington Hotel and Restaurant staff. *Photo by Roger Meekins, courtesy Outer Banks History Center.*

The Arlington advertisement. *From the private collection of Melody Leckie.*

The front of the Arlington as featured on a color postcard. *From the private collection of Melody Leckie.*

The year this was written was 1964, and if there was a family who could get a team together to make good food happen, it was Phoebe and her husband, Dewey Hayman. Talented in their own right, their ability to employ staff who were really skilled made the whole machine work.

In 1973, the ocean claimed the Arlington. Said Kathy Heinrich in a Facebook post, "We ate dinner there for my grandfather's birthday the night before the '73 nor'easter washed it out. I'll never forget going back the next day to walk there in disbelief that is could all be gone in that short of a time!"

Rum Rolls

William Smith recalled working there and loving the rolls a bit too much, "Phoebe caught me eating them just one too many times. She told me to come to work 30 minutes early the next day. She had Annie Mae make a commercial roll pan full and made me sit there and eat them all. It was years before I could even look at one again!"

2 cups sweet milk
1 cup sugar
½ cup shortening
2½ teaspoons salt
2 compressed yeast cakes
2 eggs, beaten
3 teaspoons rum extract
7 cups flour, sifted
4 tablespoons butter or margarine, melted
1½ cups seeded raisins, cut fine

Icing

2 cups confectioners sugar
4 tablespoons hot water
4 tablespoons rum extract

Pour scalded milk over ½ cup sugar, shortening and salt. Cool to lukewarm and crumble yeast into it. Beat with rotary beater until smooth. Add beaten eggs and rum extract. Add half the flour and beat with rotary until smooth. Cover with clean towel and let rise in a warm place (80–85 degrees) until double in bulk (about 3 hours). Roll dough into two strips each 12 inches long, ½ inch thick and 4 inches wide. Brush top with melted butter, and sprinkle with cup sugar and raisins. Roll up, pulling dough out at edges to keep uniform. Should be 15 inches long. Cut rolls in crosswise slices ¾ inch thick. Place in 3-inch greased muffin tins, cover with a clean towel and let rise in a warm place until double in bulk. Bake in moderately fast oven, 400 degrees or 350 for 15 to 20 minutes. As soon as rolls are removed from oven, cover with icing. Makes 36 rolls.

SEAFARE

Nags Head

Family legacy is easy to trace when following the timelines of both fine dining and the Hayman family, whose contributions to the future town of Nags Head can still be tasted.

The grandparents of modern local hotels and restaurants, the family tree that began with Phoebe and Dewey Hayman grew into an orchard. It would be fascinating to trace the genealogy. Their great-granddaughter Becky Miller is a pastry chef in her own right and has probably made more desserts than any one person ever on the Outer Banks.

Quaint oil lamps, early American furnishings and waiters in bright scarlet jackets might sound a bit kitschy these days, but they were on trend at the Seafare when it opened in 1960.

Isabel described the dining experience:

As one enters the restaurant, the cherry-paneled Seafare Room on the left is the original restaurant. The large Captain's Room on the right is the main dining room, and opening off that the Nags Head Room calls attention to an interesting diorama of Old Nags Head scenery. The food is excellent. For something really special, their Broiled Shore Dinner fills the bill with filet of fresh flounder, Backfin crabmeat, fresh shrimp aria deep sea scallops, broiled to order in lemon butter sauce. It's a real feast, not forgetting the Jumbo Imperial Crab, a seafood treat. If steak is your delight, the 12 ounce New York Sirloin, the Delmonico and T-Bone Steaks are wonderful. Seafare fried chicken, among other things, is also recommended.

Seafare servers wore bright red jackets. *From the private collection of Melody Leckie.*

Seafare staff in the dining room. *From the private collection of Melody Leckie.*

Growing up on the Outer Banks, Jen Breaux shared that she had, "so many great memories with my mom, dad, and sister at Seafare. I had my first she crab soup there. In addition to Owen's, this was our go-to restaurant."

Michelle Wagner interviewed Mike Kelly, who currently owns several local restaurants, in December 2017 for the *Restaurant Guide to the Outer Banks*. Said Kelly about his early years on the Outer Banks, "That first year, working in the kitchen at the Seafare, I enjoyed it. It kept me busy. I was given a meal a day, I had a job and a place to stay. The next year I worked in the front, starting as a busboy and then a server. I stayed in the business, got some management experience."

Kelly stayed on at Seafare, eventually becoming head waiter and assuming more and more management responsibilities. In the fall of 1972, he stayed on year-round, getting a second job building bulkheads. "Being a waiter was fun, and you had your days free," Kelly recalls. "We would fish at night, surfed a little. It was slow paced back then, there wasn't much going on—no place on the beach to get groceries or gas after 7:30, 8 at night. If you wanted a beer after work, you'd have to go over to Fred's Tavern in Manteo."

"Mike Kelly, he started at the Seafare, you know," said Manteo native Eugene Austin, "he was one of those that hired everybody, black or white, didn't matter. My mom worked for him, my aunt, my cousins. A lot of them worked at Seafare, too."

John Railey also worked at the Seafare and credits the staff with a lifelong appreciation for good food and service. Railey wrote this essay, shared with permission.

MEMORIES OF SEAFARE

by John Railey

Mike Hayman of Nags Head has been gone from this side of eternity for almost 23 years now. But those of us who loved him know he'll always have our back one way or another, just as sure as we can sit on the sand on the night of a full moon and wonder at the path of light it casts across the sea to the far horizon.

Hayman saw some of us, his staff at the Seafare restaurant, through hard times. And we witnessed his own hard times toward the end. Now, as I go through a challenging career change, I keep telling myself what Hayman, one of my mentors, would have told me: "Suck it up, bud!"

Hayman was the legendary owner/operator of the Seafare in Nags Head, which once rivaled Owens'—I contend it surpassed it for several years—as the Outer Banks' classic seafood restaurant. I make that audacious argument having graduated from years of eating at the Seafare to a few splendid years of waiting tables there in its last years, in the early 1980s.

But before I take this column out past the breakers, let me say right off that Hayman, who we called "Cap'n," was a good man but he was not a saint. Neither am I nor are many of us who strolled the magic sands of the banks and played in her waters in the good old wild days. Hayman, a Coast Guard vet who was a master sailor and fisherman, was, to put it politely, mercurial, even for those rowdy days.

He was loyal to his workers but he demanded the best from us and could go on a tirade if we didn't deliver, even if we were "treed"—our language for hustling to keep up with too many tables. Hayman wouldn't cut loose in the dining rooms, but he would let us know in the back halls that he was displeased. We called his anger "The Blunt" or "The Big Eye." It was not pretty. I withered under his hurricanes. But I got tougher.

And he could charm us workers as well as he could his customers. He was beach royalty, the son of parents who owned and operated the Arlington hotel at Milepost 13 on the Beach Road. They started an oyster bar across the road from their hotel. In the late 1960s, Hayman enlarged that oyster bar and transformed it into the Seafare, an oasis of pink stucco in the sand in the midst of The Unpainted Aristocracy, those venerable cottages of cedar shake.

Hayman, who attended N.C. State, worked his dining rooms like an old-school ambassador, as at ease with the northeastern North Carolina aristocrats as he was with patrons of modest means and with those of new money from elsewhere, making them all feel like he was their best friend. He was a big man with brown hair, a boyish face and a charming grin, dressed in a blazer, khakis and Topsiders sans socks, beach-style.

He taught me much about restaurants, working with all sorts of people and about working hard in general. Before I left the beach, Hayman lost the Seafare through an unjust deed manipulation, then the restaurant burned down in August 1984. Hayman worked a variety of jobs, won a suit involving the old restaurant with the help of former Seafare-waiter-turned-lawyer-Everett Thompson II and sprang back with a new Seafare in a building behind the spot where his old restaurant had stood. I visited

A Seafare advertisement in *Surfside News*, July, 1977. *From the private collection of Melody Leckie.*

Hayman and some of his family there and we'd talk about old times, the good old times. He encouraged me in my journalism career.

He died of a heart attack at his Nags Head home in May 1995. He was only 51.

I thought about him often, especially when I reported on Hurricane Isabel from the Outer Banks in September 2003. Hayman would have loved being in the middle of that wild mix with me.

I think about him still and his courageous outlook on his career and those of his former employees, through all our changes. I am sucking it up, Cap'n, in your best tradition. The far horizon at the end of that full moon's path awaits.

—*John Railey is the former editorial page editor of the* Winston-Salem Journal

Seafood Chowder

Serves 12

5 thick slices streak of lean and streak of fat
¼ cup butter
½ cup finely diced onions
½ cup finely diced celery
½ pound mushrooms, sliced
1 quart milk
1 pint heavy cream
1 teaspoon salt
¼ teaspoon black pepper
1 whole lemon rind, grated or minced
2 pinches ground basil
4 dozen shucked oysters
4 dozen shucked sea scallops
1 pound lump crab meat (check for shell and remove if any)
1 pound, 40–50 shrimp, shelled and deveined
1 bunch parsley, chopped
4 ounces sherry wine

Sauté the lean and fat in butter with the onions, celery and mushrooms until lightly browned. Stir in milk, cream and spices and bring to a slow boil. Simmer on low heat. Add seafood and cook until shrimp are done. Stir constantly. Finish with parsley and sherry wine.

Horseradish Sauce

¼ pound butter
¼ cup flour
1 quart milk
¼ teaspoon onion powder
4 cloves, crushed
¼ teaspoon salt
¼ teaspoon salt
¼ teaspoon red pepper
4 tablespoons whipped cream
3 tablespoons dry mustard

3 tablespoons vinegar
2 teaspoons sugar
3 tablespoons sherry
1 cup horseradish

Melt butter in saucepan; add flour and mix well. Stir over medium heat constantly, until thick paste forms. Add small amounts of milk, stirring after each addition. As mixture thickens, each time, add a little more milk slowly until lumps disappear. Continue stirring and adding milk until all milk has been used.

Remove saucepan from heat and add the remaining ingredients in order given. Horseradish sauce is now ready to serve at room temperature. The sauce can also be stored in a container in the refrigerator for up to two weeks. When need arises, the sauce can be removed from the refrigerator and heated slowly over low heat before serving. (Perfect for grilled fish!)

Hot Crabmeat Dip

For a party of 12

2 pounds Philadelphia cream cheese
2 cups sour cream
4 tablespoons chopped scallions
¼ cup minced green peppers (par cooked)
¼ cup minced onions
1 good dash of salt
1 good pinch of white pepper
Juice from 2 lemons
Dash of Tabasco sauce
2 bunches chopped parsley
2 pounds lump crab meat (check for shell and remove if any)
1 cup slivered almonds

Using a double boiler, heat the cream cheese and sour cream until warm. Add the chopped scallions, peppers, onions and heat for 10 minutes. Now add the salt, pepper, lemon juice and hot sauce and heat for 10 minutes.

Add the parsley flakes and fold in the crab meat (careful to leave many of the lumps). Now add the almonds and let stand in a chafing dish for 10 minutes before serving. Place a large assortment of crackers around to dip in the hot crab dip.

Chocolate Pecan Pie

2 ounces chocolate
3 tablespoons butter
1 cup light corn syrup
¾ cup sugar
3 eggs
1 teaspoon vanilla
1 ¼ cups pecans
1 pie shell

Melt chocolate with butter. Cool. Melt corn syrup with sugar; cool. Beat eggs slightly; add to syrup mixture. Add the cooled chocolate. Stir in the vanilla and pecans. Bake in pie shell for 35–40 minutes at 325 degrees.

Note: Pecan pie—Follow same above ingredients and directions, except omit the chocolate and the butter.

One of the original sun-faded Seafare signs. *Photo by the author.*

ELEGANT PELICAN

Nags Head

Summertime sunsets can be unanticipated treats for first-time diners on the Outer Banks. Expecting fabulous sunrises over the Atlantic, many hungry travelers are surprised to learn that we also have westward-facing eateries and that they can be the perfect spots for watching the sun disappear into the horizon, especially while sipping and noshing.

The property now known as Pamlico Jack's Pirate Hideaway, in Nags Head, features a breathtaking view of grassy salt marshes and the nearby Albemarle Sound from an extra-large deck, now adorned with an authentically replicated pirate ship that houses the Run Jumpers Bar.

Conveniently, the time of the daily sunset is usually posted on the marquee, and that is what has always been a selling point for this location.

Originally operated as the Elegant Pelican, owned by chef and operator Arthur Sturges, the restaurant was managed by Carlen Pearl, who went on to open Colington Café, and Chef Cary Vanischak, who later led the kitchen team at Windmill Point.

Captain Cheesecake, also known as Arthur Sturges, owned and operated the Elegant Pelican in Nags Head. The restaurant was managed by Carlen Pearl, who went on to open the Colington Café, and Cary Vanischak, who went on to lead the kitchen team at Windmill Point. *Photo by Drew C. Wilson, courtesy Outer Banks History Center.*

"Elegant Pelican became Penguin Isle," Richard Willis remembered on Facebook, "Art was used to catering to a appreciative, wealthy clientele. He knew all the great chefs of that time and they visited and sometimes would cook. Captain Cheesecake, as he was known, could create desserts to die for."

There are various reasons folks give for the closure of Elegant Pelican, laughed Willis, "He did not shut down as much as take the money and run. Was not happy and got a good offer from one of our local restaurateurs. I remember one night being there late in the evening and he came over and sat with us. He said if one more tourist asked why they could not have a baked potato he was going to, well let's say explode."

Elegant Pelican's Pasta D'Angelo recipe was shared by Marsha Johnson, who said, "Arthur Sturges was a fun guy to work for. Here is a recipe he gave me. He was never shy about sharing his love for food. His wife Ellen Sturges was wonderful too."

She added, "This recipe was so good, I make it often with Shrimp. There is not a lot of detailed instructions on this recipe."

Elegant Pelican's Pasta D'Angelo

Sauté together olive oil and real butter. Add onion, tomatoes, mushrooms, big time amount of garlic, black olives. Simmer. Add scallops, shrimp, crab or combination. Cook seafood. Finish with a handful of chopped basil. Toss with angel hair pasta and plate.

Some say that he also added lots of cracked black pepper.

PENGUIN ISLE

Mike Kelly bought Elegant Pelican after its second year in operation and changed the name to Penguin Isle. The sound-side sunsets were still a main attraction, and every table had a view; there was a gentle remodel, and the windows in the dining room were made even more expansive. Chef Lee Miller took over the kitchen, and Doug Tutweiler managed the dining room.

Popular dishes were the duck confit and the grilled game fish of the day. The wine list grew, and Wine Spectator awards were garnered. Penguin Isle

Doug Tutweiler changes the lettering on the sign at Penguin Isle Soundside Restaurant and Bar during Hurricane Bob. Penguin Isle was known for posting the nightly sunset time on its marquee. The sunset view was, of course, fabulous from the restaurant and back deck. *Photo by Drew C. Wilson, courtesy Outer Banks History Center.*

also had a raspberry vinaigrette for the salad that came with every meal; it was a thick emulsion, almost creamy, and was particularly popular. The kitchen team also baked a variety of fresh breads daily, including some sort of daily fruit bread that people absolutely craved. A basket of the various breads was complimentary for every table.

The team hosted popular buffets on Easter and Thanksgiving that featured a variety of dishes made from fresh seafood as well as traditional holiday fare like ham and turkey. There were always plenty of sides, too, like cornbread and sweet potatoes.

The Kelly restaurant team decided to try a new concept and changed the theme to pirate and the menu to casual; it is now called Pamlico Jacks.

Shrimp Aristotle with Scallion Fettuccine

From Chef Lee Miller, this was one of the most popular recipes on the menu at Penguin Isle

Serves 4

1 cup heavy cream
Salt and pepper, to taste

1 large tomato, diced
1 green bell pepper, julienned
8 mushrooms, sliced
1–2 tablespoons minced fresh garlic
1 zucchini squash, julienned
1 ½ pounds large shrimp, peeled and deveined
½ pound fresh scallion fettuccine or store-bought fettuccine
½ pound fresh scallion fettuccine or store-bought fettuccine
4 ounces feta cheese, crumbled
1 tablespoon water
Green onions, for garnish
2 teaspoons olive oil

Simmer cream until reduced to ⅔ cup or slightly thickened, do not let boil over side of pot. Season reduced cream with salt and pepper, cook for 30 seconds. Add all vegetables and shrimp and cook; add water to keep from burning. Cook until shrimp are pink and the vegetables are hot. Cook homemade fettuccine or fresh store-bought pasta until al dente (30–45 seconds). Toss drained pasta with butter and olive oil and divide equally between four warm serving bowls. Top pasta with reduced cream and feta cheese and the remaining shrimp and vegetable mixture. Serve immediately, garnish with green onions.

Scallion Fettuccine
Serves 8

½ cup tightly packed spinach, washed
½ cup green onions, 1 inch pieces
1 tablespoon olive oil
2 teaspoons salt
3 large eggs
3¼ cups all-purpose flour
Cornmeal
3 tablespoons butter

Puree spinach and green onions in a food processor with olive oil and 1 teaspoon salt. Add eggs and combine for a couple of seconds. Add flour and combine until thoroughly mixed; scrape bottom and sides with a

The low-key back deck of Penguin Isle Soundside Bar and Restaurant was a simple stage over the marsh and the star was the sunset. *Photo by the author.*

spatula. Note: if pasta dough does not stay together or crumbles, add ½ teaspoon water until it does form a uniform ball of dough. Cover with plastic wrap for one hour or overnight to allow dough to rest. After cutting fettuccine, toss with 2–3 tablespoons of cornmeal to prevent pasta from sticking together. Cook in boiled salted water for 30 seconds to one minute until al dente. Toss fettuccine with butter.

WINDMILL POINT

Nags Head

Chef Cary Vanischak started working for Dr. Sarah Forbes at Windmill Point after his run at Elegant Pelican, and together they fed thousands. He did so while leading her kitchen though seasons of elegant, sound-side dining surrounded by salvaged artifacts from a decommissioned ship.

An ad in the 1989 issue of *Outer Banks Magazine* declared that Windmill Point Restaurant and the United States Lounge remained open year-round, seven days a week. Not many places were at that time. Seasonality was the reason the Outer Banks came to be in the first place.

The ad continued, "Casual, fine waterfront dining, featuring steaks and one of the area's largest seafood selections. The perfect complement to this unique dining experience includes your favorite beverage and a spectacular view of the Roanoke Sound with its unparalleled sunsets, from the United States Lounge."

Lee Ann Bruders worked behind the original bar from the SS *United States*. The entire upstairs piano bar lounge was filled with memorabilia, as was the downstairs dining room at Windmill Point. *Photo by Drew C. Wilson, courtesy Outer Banks History Center.*

The salvaged décor was, in a way, modern-day pirate, only the parts and pieces used to decorate the restaurant cost owner Dr. Sarah Forbes a pretty purse. If you were into ships, it was kind of a big deal to have all the stuff Windmill Point had.

Dr. Forbes bragged, "We hold more memorabilia from the S.S. *United States* than any other private collection." And she did. She bought it all at an auction in 1984.

The restaurant was chock-full of as much memorabilia as she could place; it even had the authentic kidney-shaped bar and furnishings from the ship upstairs in the lounge. The piano was one of a kind and was made from fire-resistant wood. The original designs had called for it to be made of aluminum. Fire resistance was a trend at the time the ship was built in the early 1950s; the SS *United States* had its maiden voyage in 1952 and sailed until 1969.

Forbes was also quite proud of the namesake windmill; her ad also boasted, "As for our windmill, it has great beauty. Having been constructed from century old trees by a craftsman brought over from England, it is also one of a kind."

The soundfront dining room of Windmill Point Restaurant in Nags Head was one of the most thematic eateries the Outer Banks has ever known. The entire upstairs piano bar lounge was filled with memorabilia from the SS *United States*, as were the downstairs dining room and the lobby. *Photo by the author.*

Windmill Point Lounge with the fireproof piano and other memorabilia from the SS *United States*. *Photo by the author.*

Windmill Point's dining room, in the last year of operation, prepared for dinner service. The patriotic décor was a hit with visitors, who often dressed to match the red, white and blue theme that went along with the memorabilia from the SS *United States*. *Photo by the author.*

SS *United States* memorabilia covered everything at Windmill Point except the kitchen doors. *Photo by the author.*

Dr. Forbes had a reputation as a formidable yet benevolent businesswoman. She led both regional hospitals and local construction projects with equal zeal and determination. She was a lover of animals, children and women's causes. She also preserved history by acquiring, through her trust, a collection of real estate properties. The rental management team donates profits from the rentals to local charities benefiting Dr. Forbes's favorite causes.

EL GAY RESTAURANT

Nags Head

The El Gay was named after the original owners' children, Eddie Lee and Gayle Brown. Eddie and Irene Brown, who owned and operated El Gay, built a reputation for good food and service. They used only local fresh seafood, and their jumbo shrimp, soft-shell crabs and crab cakes were house specialties.

Eddie was the chef, and when the Browns opened in the mid-1950s, the El Gay advertised in the *Coastland Times*. The ads boasted fountain service and boxed lunches, which were popular for beachgoers and fishermen.

The restaurant was on the south side of the El Gay Motor Court, which later became the Manor Motel.

Said Pamela Coleburn on the Outer Banks Vintage Scrapbook webpage, "Ate many times at the El Gay Restaurant back in the 50's & 60's. The owner was a cook in the Navy in WW2. Cooked a mean fried blue fish!"

From Isabel Murphy in 1964:

> *The dinner menu carries an interesting choice of delicious foods, and for a start, their home-made chicken soup is as much in demand as the shrimp cocktail. Most all seashore visitors want seafood, and to fill that bill, there's soft shell crabs, ocean scallops, fish fresh from Outer Banks waters, fresh Nags Head crabmeat cakes and a combination seafood platter containing a variety of select seafood, all served with French fries, tossed salad, cole slaw, lettuce and tomatoes, hot rolls and beverage.*

Murphy detailed the menu extensively:

> *El Gay's roast beef dinner includes fresh greens also, and their Rib-I Steak, fried chicken with fresh green peas, are favorites with diners. Cold plates*

Left: El Gay Restaurant was next door to the El Gay Motor Court and was named after the owners' children. *Photo by Aycock Brown, courtesy Outer Banks History Center.*

Below: Mermaid Food Shop, across from the El Gay Restaurant and Motel, on the beach road in Nags Head. *Photo by Roger Meekins, courtesy Outer Banks History Center.*

include baked Smithfield Ham with potato salad and sliced tomatoes. The baked sugar-cured ham is served with buttered parsley potatoes, fresh green string beans, French fries, hot rolls, coffee or tea. They also serve fresh-cooked corned beef among other good things.

She went on:

Their prices are moderate and the service at El Gay is fast and courteous. In case you want an early breakfast, they're open at 6:30 every morning and I'm sure you will enjoy the fried or broiled country ham and country fresh eggs to go with it. North Carolina grits too, in fact El Gay was one of the first restaurants on the beach to serve grits. It's as famous a breakfast dish in North Carolina as the fried potatoes of the West. A hearty breakfast starts the day off right, and as a day-starter you just can't beat good hot coffee as you'll have it at El Gay.

The Browns eventually sold the property. Said local historian Melody Leckie, "It was the El Gay Motor Court, renamed Gay Motor Court and then finally became the Manor Motel which was torn down in 2011."

Maryann Maryott added,

My husband and I owned and operated this as the Manor Motel from 1990 until 2004 when we sold it to someone who said he was going to run it for a few years and then build 2 rental homes on the property. We really enjoyed our years welcoming families who had been staying there for many years. We did our best to make it a friendly and fun place and kept it in the best condition we could despite the aging of the structures. Now there are 2 Mega mansions where our charming cottage court once stood. Sad to see the end of a wonderful era!

THE CAROLINIAN

Nags Head

"I always thought the Carolinian was the most beautiful building on the beach. When I walked through, it was awesome," shared Roy Wescott on Outer Banks Vintage Scrapbook, "Years later the inside and rooms had

An aerial view of the Carolinian Hotel was the subject of a postcard by Dan C. Morrill. *From the private collection of Melody Leckie.*

aged out and I couldn't believe how old and outdated it had become. Still, a monument!"

Cliff Blakely agreed, "It was built in a different time. Time when guests only used their rooms to sleep and change clothes. All socializing was done in the huge 1st and 2nd floor rooms with other guests. The guest rooms were tiny compared to today's standards."

An Outer Banks landmark, the Carolinian Hotel first opened in the summer of 1947 between Mile Post 10 and 11, on the Beach Road in Nags Head. It was one of the iconic hotels considered Outer Banks royalty. The property changed hands many times, but the social scene was always present. Dining, cocktails, dancing and repeat were the daily routine of guests at the seaside inn.

Early on in the hotel's history, Carl Goerch praised the on-site eatery in his 1949 book, *Pitchin' Tar: A Compilation of Facts Concerning Various Things You Will Find in North Carolina*: "We recommend the Carolinian Hotel. It is open year 'round. Crab royal is their specialty. Ask for it."

In an October 6, 1958 *Sports Illustrated* article, "Down the Banks to Ocracoke," Virginia Kraft wrote,

The Dogwood Room at the Carolinian Hotel. This Oceanside dining room featured its namesake motif on the wallpaper. *Photo by Roger Meekins, courtesy Outer Banks History Center.*

At Nags Head The Carolinian Hotel ($10 and up per day, American plan) remains open all year, and this is the local headquarters for sportsmen. Inside, a fire is usually burning in the wood paneled Anchor Club where, at the end of the day, guests shelter against the evening's chill. At this time of year, the talk is always of sport—deer hunting, surf fishing, fox chasing—but mainly of geese and ducks.

Isabel Murphy wrote,

The Carolinian on the oceanfront at Nags Head, is one of the mid-Atlantic's most complete motor hotels. Air conditioned and carpeted, the Carolinian contains 94 guest rooms, each with private tile baths, telephones and every modern comfort. The colonial-type cottages are located within the hotel compound and contain spacious rooms and suites. Private sundecks overlook the ocean, beach and surrounding scenery. The two swimming pools are protected by walls for privacy and comfort.

The Carolinian's air conditioned dining rooms seat more than 200 diners. Window walls in both the Driftwood and Dogwood rooms, provide a panoramic view of the rolling surf and 'all the ships at sea. The Sea

119

Oaks deck. Perched atop an oceanside dune, adjoins the main dining room and is popular in summer for alfresco dining and teatime refreshment.

Yaupon tea, an ancient Outer Banks beverage, is a specialty of the Carolinian and as famous hereabouts as the gourd-sipped mate of South America. Long before coffee or China tea was in use on these Outer Banks islands, yaupon was the Outer Banker's "cup of tea." All one had to do in those days was to gather the leaves from the native shrub, cure them and brew the tea. The Carolinian is following the old-time custom of serving youpon.

Food at the Carolinian is prepared and served with loving care, as you'll agree when you taste their seafood bisque, for instance. It contains a variety of seafoods of the area and is a taste treat in Dare coast dining; also lobster Newburg, deviled crabs and broiled bluefish. For something different there's swordfish fresh from the sea, as are all seafoods served at the Carolinian, and the Carolinian's roast beef has the blessing of gourmets and is bathed lavishly in its own delicious juices. All breads are homebaked and the Sally Lunn, in loaf or muffins, is really special. Breakfast goodies there include country ham, cornmeal griddle cakes served with fish roe, eggs, and among other things, mighty good coffee. The Carolinian's pecan pies are made from an old family recipe and so good! Tipsy cake and other choice desserts await your choosing.

Murphy finished, "The hotel's Anchor Club is a gathering place where friends and guests meet for conversation and conviviality. The marine decor of ship's lanterns, life rings and other nautical appointments, contribute to a shipboard feeling, and when the sun gets over the yardarm you'll want to be aboard. With live music on Saturday evenings, it's a time to be merry."

Dr. Henry Vanderbilt Johnson saw the Carolinian from a different perspective as he noted in his book *Kronicles of a Kolored Kid*:

One of the major assets of working at the Carolinian Motel and Restaurant was the availability of housing. The management provided dishwashers, waiters, waitresses, cooks, bus boys, and other workers with lodging in the basement of the motel. To this end, we did not have to spend extra money for rent and utilities. Working at the Carolinian was an absolute divine blessing. I had a warm and clean place to work, plenty of good and healthy food, and the beach was within five minutes from my bed.

Alan Peterson was the main cook at the Carolinian and he always treated me like a younger brother He actually had a younger brother that everyone called Duck, I never knew Duck's real name; however, he was

An unidentified couple enjoying the Carolinian's relaxed summer vibe and on-site restaurant. *Photo by Aycock Brown, courtesy Outer Banks History Center.*

equally as nice to me as his brother. Alan and Duck were originally from Hyde County; as such, they referred to me as homeboy.

Even though I could walk to the beach within five minutes from my living quarters, I really did not spend a great amount of time in the water or roaming the beach. Seemingly, the beach was not a place for black people or other minorities. In fact, I seldom ever saw blacks combing the beaches like white Americans. I never saw black surfers or black hotel managers. The only blacks that I ever saw in Nags Head were the ones working in fancy restaurants or motels. Nags Head appeared to be a great escape for middle class and upper class rich white Americans. Blacks traditionally gravitated to the area to work and to pay bills. Nags Head definitely was not a utopia for black Americans; nevertheless, it was an oasis for summer employment. I simply loved each summer experience and in most cases, the summer could not come fast enough. Working in Nags Head was equally as exciting as Christmas. It was filled with mystery, excitement and anticipation....

There were no black clubs on the beach. There were no designated black hangouts or black-owned businesses. Blacks who worked on the beach had to travel to Manteo for social entertainment and fun activities.

By 1988, the hotel had definitely lost its luster, but the music lived on. The Carolinian was mostly known for holding concerts, often of the reggae variety. How times had changed. Larry Fox wrote in the *Washington Post*,

The only place we found that served up serious music was the Carolinian Hotel, a funky oceanfront establishment with a paneled second-floor lobby complete with parrot. The Carolinian nightclub serves up comedy or music by name bands. What's the room like? Dunno: The only people jam we encountered was here, and we couldn't get in. In short, enjoy the sun and surf and go to bed early. Or get to the Carolinian early.

The Carolinian Hotel was demolished in 2001 to make way for several luxury beachfront residences.

Carolinian Griddle Cakes
Cornmeal Griddle Cakes

¾ cup white cornmeal
3 tablespoons shortening
1 ½ cups boiling water.
1 ¼ cups sweet milk
3 eggs
2 tablespoons molasses or 1 tablespoon sugar
1 ½ teaspoons salt
1 ½ cups flour
1 ½ tablespoons baking powder

Mix cornmeal, shortening and water and let stand 5 minutes to cool. Add milk, eggs, sweetener and dry ingredients. Beat all ingredients well together. Bake on a hot greased griddle, turning to brown on both sides. Cook a little more slowly than regular griddle cakes. Serve with butter and honey, molasses or syrup. These are especially good with the herring roe or salt fish. (Recipe makes 24 cakes of medium size.)

DARE-O-LINA RESTAURANT

Nags Head

The Dare-o-lina Restaurant, which adjoined the Sea Oatel in Nags Head was known as a "pink palace" of fine foods. Two glass-walled dining rooms, one overlooking the ocean, the other with a view of the Roanoke Sound and Roanoke Island, drew customers from all over the beach.

Specials such as baked bluefish stuffed with crab meat, soft-shell crabs, stuffed shrimp, seafood casserole, fish fried or broiled, crab or shrimp sautéed in butter were the draw. All the seafood was just-from-the-boat fresh.

Above: Dare-o-lina Restaurant, in Nags Head. *Photo by Roger Meekins, courtesy Outer Banks History Center.*

Left: Dare-o-lina Restaurant advertisement, from *Surfside News*, 1967. *From the private collection of Melody Leckie.*

Dare-o-lina Restaurant advertisement from *Surfside News*, 1977. *From the private collection of Melody Leckie.*

Clam Chowder

The clam chowder at Dare-o-lina was especially popular and is made in the traditional Outer Banks style, with no cream or tomatoes.

1 cup diced salt pork
6 potatoes
1 medium onion, chopped
1 quart clam broth
Salt and pepper, to taste
Chopped clams
Cornmeal, to thicken

Slice salt pork and fry in heavy frying pan. Add pork cracklings to potatoes, onions and clam broth. Add salt and pepper to taste. Boil 45 minutes, add chopped clams and continue to cook for 15 minutes. Thicken with cornmeal to consistency desired.

3

Roanoke Island and Mainland Dare County

The area now known as Roanoke Island was once known as Nags Head. Pretty much everything east of Columbia was called Nags Head, especially if the words were coming from a traveler. Over time, Manteo, Wanchese, Skyco, Manns Harbor, East Lake and Stumpy Point all carved out unique and quaint neighborhoods and are now more collectively known as Roanoke Island.

The county seat is in Manteo, meaning the courthouse and associated businesses and governmental agencies are there. Lunchtime food trade has always been popular; it was a time for community, to see and be seen, to catch up on the news, so many eateries were located in the "downtown" area surrounding the courthouse.

The downtown waterfront was one of the first areas developed in the town, as was the northwest side, where you will still find the historically black neighborhoods and homes built by descendants of former slaves. "Roanoke Island is home to the Freedmen's Colony," notes Patricia Click on her website, roanokefreedmenscolony.com, which is dedicated to telling the story of a camp for newly freed slaves:

> *During the Civil War, Union-occupied Roanoke Island, which lies between the North Carolina mainland and the barrier islands known as the Outer Banks, became home to thousands of former slaves.*
>
> *Initially these refugees settled near the Union headquarters, creating a community that included churches and a school. In the spring of 1863, this camp evolved into a government-sanctioned colony. Major General*

John G. Foster, Commander of the 18th Army Corps, ordered Horace James, a Congregational minister from New England who was serving as a chaplain in the Union army, to establish a colony of former slaves on the island. Although the Roanoke Island freedmen's colony was an experiment of national significance, few people are aware of its history.

At one point, it is estimated that the population of the Freedman's Colony grew to over three thousand people. Kathleen Angione wrote about Click and her book in *Coast Watch*:

When the Confederacy collapsed in April 1865, the Union returned all land to owners who held title. The Freedmen now faced eviction. But just as they labored to build their colony, the Freedmen labored to keep it—or at least some of it. A small group petitioned the government, requesting to rent the land where their homes stood. In 1868, 11 petitioners scraped together $500 and bought 200 acres of land from the heirs of Thomas Dough, according to Click.

By 1900, only 300 black residents lived on the island, in a neighborhood called "California." That year, the government divided the property into 11 lots, based on the original buyers and their heirs.

This California Road sign is one of the few markers designating a neighborhood on the west side of Roanoke Island. Miss Esther's place was near this intersection. *Photo by the author.*

The black community grew, independent of and isolated from the white population except for a few occasions, court, a few eateries with mixed clientele and late-night escapades on Good Luck Street and the juke joints on the north side of town. By the mid-century, Jim Crow had effectively divided local communities, and when laws eventually changed, it did not mean that local behavior changed quickly.

While most locals interviewed about this era said that there were few actual signs designating where blacks could or could not eat, many remembered that there were places that were less safe for blacks to venture and neighbors shared with one another where blacks were and were not welcome.

Linwood Delroy Bowser remembers having to go to the back door of a prominent local restaurant to order food. He could order and pay but could not eat inside. These were complicated times. Blacks were necessary employees of many of the mentioned establishments, but were not always welcomed into the dining rooms as customers. This is a practice that lasted into the late 1960s and early 1970s, just a very short time ago.

The Lost Colony is the colony that is more frequently mentioned on Roanoke Island; it is a fictional play, presented as an outdoor drama, that tells a tale of the first English settlers and their integration into the country. The performances are held during the summer, and talented local and visiting actors dramatize a story of colonists gone missing. Paul Green wrote the play, which draws thousands of visitors to the area each year, and since it was first staged in 1937, Roanoke Island restaurants have graciously marketed suppers to ticket holders so they could make it to the show on time.

BOARDINGHOUSES OF LILA SIMMONS AND CORDELIA WISE

Lila Simmons Tourist Home
Manteo

Visionaries, entrepreneurs, feeders and best friends Lila Ashby Simmons and Cordelia Wise each opened a boardinghouse on the west side of Roanoke Island to take in workers. Lila's place was called Lila Simmons Tourist Home and she offered room, board and nurturing hospitality to visiting workers. The travelers were contracted to provide trade services throughout Nags Head and the workforce contributed to the the building of local bridges, but there was no place for them to spend the night. Hotels were thriving on the beach, just not for blacks.

"She was the best business woman in the whole wide world," Lila's granddaughter, retired educator and Dare County commissioner and School Board Member Virginia Simmons Tillett recalled. "I can remember when I was 10–11 years old, my grandmother and her friend Cordelia started their Bed and Breakfasts because folks would come to work in Nags Head and didn't have any place to stay. So, they started taking in boarders."

"You could always go there and buy a sandwich or a soda, too." Virginia said, "Cordelia Wise's place was next to where the Ace Hardware is now. You could go there and get any meal, too."

Entrepreneurs were everywhere, and Tillett smiled as she remembered, "Miss Elizabeth 'Lizzie' Barber sold ice cream during the summer. She charged a penny, that was how she made extra money." It was always vanilla and went from being served in a cup to being served in a cone when ice cream cones became commercially available. "We didn't have restaurants, we had places called cafes or luncheonettes, we had places called shops where you could hang out, dance, play dominoes. When I was in middle school and high school, we would hang out at Lucy's Corner, everyone did." "There were places on the North End, too, near where the airport is now, they were for the Black Navy men who needed a place to, you know, hang out," said Virginia. The Civil Air Patrol camp was on the north side, by the airport, and many of the servicemen were black.

That is where Nick's House of Joy was located. "Nick Meekins was the first black to have a television and it was in his juke joint. It was a big ol' RCA and everyone would get together over there and watch the fights. He would tell all the children, 'gimme ten cents,' that's how he got 'em to stay quiet, see, gimme ten cents and when the fight is over, if you were quiet, you get your ten cents back," Delroy Bowser laughed.

The Civil Air Patrol brought black pilots to the Outer Banks, and many of them needed a place to stay, eat and hang out. Local entrepreneurs like Lila Simmons and Cordelia Wise stepped up and filled the gaps. *Photo by the author.*

Left: Tourist Home owner Lila Simmons was an expert feather plucker, among her many other entrepreneurial talents. Here she is cleaning a goose brought to her from a recent hunt. She would clean the birds and use the down feathers to make pillows. *Right*: Legendary commercial fisherman Snooks Tillett repairs one of his many fishing nets. This work was always done by hand. *Courtesy of Virginia Tillett Collection.*

Virginia also remembered a first. "Lila Simmons was the first person in our neighborhood with a phone and she would charge 5 cents for a call. She also started the first sort of thrift store on her porch. She was also a professional cleaner of ducks and geese, she saved the feathers for pillows," Virginia smiled, "she could do anything. She'd tell me I could, too. I can still hear her tell me 'hold that head up and those shoulders back.'"

"Let's just say, we knew where we could dip our feet," said Virginia when asked about segregation, and "there were definitely places we didn't go to eat. So, we had our own places, like Lila Simmons' place."

Today, Virginia Tillett lives only a few blocks away from the two tracts that her ancestors inherited, in the home where she and her husband raised their two sons. The act of owning land in Dare County was, and still is, a pretty big deal. Restricted covenants in some beach areas prevented sale of property to blacks until the 1968 Fair Housing Act declared them unconstitutional. "Remember," added Virginia Tillett, "in 1868, Blacks in Dare County did purchase land, that is how my family did it."

Virginia Tillett's parents, Earlene Simmons and William Seward Simmons, and her paternal grandmother, Lila, dedicated their lives to food. Her mom picked crabs for over thirty years at Daniel's seafood, and her dad retired from the National Park Service.

Her husband, William "Snooks" Tillett, was a legendary commercial fisherman, and his father, Joe Tillett, once had the largest farm in Dare County. "Snooks Tillett was raised on a multi acre farm and they raised and sold vegetables, well, everything else, too. It was a working farm. We had chickens, cows, pigs. Even had mills. We always had fresh vegetables on the table," Virginia reminisced, "in the summer we always had something sliced from the garden…cucumbers, tomatoes. Of course, there was always fresh seafood."

Shared Snooks's cousin, Linwood Delroy Bowser, "Snooks was a legend for blacks. After him, no one took up fishing."

Restaurant owner and former state senator Marc Basnight (*left*) hugs neighbors Virginia and Snooks Tillett, all longtime friends and supporters of the local restaurant industry. Virginia began working in Walkers Diner as a young woman and went on to become a member of the county school board and a Dare County commissioner. Snooks was a commercial fisherman who provided local eateries with fresh from the boat seafood. Basnight became the owner of Banight's Lone Cedar Café. *Courtesy of Virginia Tillett Collection.*

Above: Collins Park is located on Sir Walter Raleigh, formerly known as Good Luck Street, the site of several beloved boardinghouses, shops, cafés and juke joints. *Photo by the author.*

Left: The original cookhouse from the Pea Island Life Saving Station has been preserved and is located in Collins Park in Manteo. *Photo by the author.*

Snooks Tillett was a beloved Manteo waterman, skilled at navigating more than just the local waters. In the days "before the Jim Crow era, blacks dominated many of the state's maritime trades and lived in every coastal area," said author David Cecelski in his essay series *The Color of Water*. "In nearly every part of the North Carolina coast, their skills as swimmers, fishermen and boatmen were legendary. That attachment to our coastal waters was sorely tested during the Jim Crow era: Nags Head, Carolina Beach and Wrightsville Beach were typical of white beach resorts and beachfront towns on the North Carolina coast."

"Some of those, like Nags Head," reminded Cecelski, "were very old beach resorts. Even before the Civil War, the white cottagers at Nags Head kept the ocean beaches off-limits to people of color, except for one hour late every summer afternoon."

Fried Spots

This is a recipe shared by Virginia Tillett, and it works for herring, too, that were salted the previous season. "I can hear my grandmother say, 'bring in 10 of those spots' we'd go out to the storage house where we kept vegetables and canned goods. The fish were in barrels. We would buy big bags of salt and cover the fish during season. So, when we brought them in we would soak them overnight, before we cooked them."

Pull spot from salt barrel 24 hours before intended meal. Soak in water to remove some of the salt; change the water a few times. Dredge the fish in cornmeal and fry in oil or lard in a cast-iron skillet until extra crispy. Note: Sometimes the people interviewed called extra crispy "fried hard."

MISS ESTHER'S

Manteo

"It's ok, you can call it soul food. That's what it is," said Virginia Tillett as we sat at her kitchen table sipping coffee and talking about the type of food the cafés on the west and north sides of Roanoke Island served.

Miss Esther's is what most people called Esther Govan's place on the west side of Manteo. She had a cookhouse next door to her brick home. When she wasn't at the shop, the hungry could knock on her side door and she would answer and come out and make them a plate of food. *Photo by the author.*

The menu at Miss Esther's changed daily and always featured whatever she wanted to cook. The ingredients were predominately locally sourced and seasonal. The food must have been some kind of good. When asked about exact dishes, her most satisfied guests all seemed to start their answers with deep groans, as if their stomachs remembered the deliciousness first. As the eye-rolling moans turned into smiles, the words usually started forming.

Local chef, friend and fan Lovey Selby said of Miss Esther's:

> *Her most famous dish was called yak, it was a spicy noodle dish with red sauce and chicken or pork. Pigs feet. Collards with cornmeal dumplings. Anything southern, she cooked and it was delish.*
>
> *She also cooked dumplings made with flour, baking powder, salt, butter, and milk. Cornmeal dumplings in collards the same way just add cornmeal. Everything cooked was always in a cast iron skillet. Fried spots, biscuits, beans, you name it. It was most definitely cooked in a cast iron skillet. Catfish stew, turtle stew. All made with love and salt pork meat, and of course, bacon grease! Fried spots was always cooked with the heads on so crispy when eatin, nothing was left but the spine. Mmmmmm.*

Esther Daniels Govan, who passed away in 1986, when she was seventy-three, operated that legendary little eatery in Manteo for years, and she was a natural-born feeder known to fix a plate of food even if she wasn't open. If she was home, next door to her café, all you had to do was call to her and she would come out and make sure you were fed.

Miss Esther's was located on Good Luck Street, now renamed Sir Walter Raleigh. For many years, Good Luck Street was the place to meet and be met. Lucy's Corner, LaVada's Juke Joint and David Latham's Nightspot were also located on Good Luck Street. According to Dr. Henry V. Johnson, author of *Kronicles of a Kolored Kid*, they were the places to be on Friday, Saturday and Sunday nights, "Black folks would put on their Sunday best just to be a part of the crowd." In his book, Dr. Johnson recalls that blacks were allowed to work in Nags Head at places like the Casino, but they were not welcome to party after work. "Typically, after the Casino closed, workers would rush to Good Luck Street," explained Johnson.

"Well, there was at least one time that the Casino let in blacks and that was because of Fats Domino," said local resident Eugene Austin, "That's right. Fats Domino refused to play unless they let blacks in. So, that night, they did. We all dressed up and had a big time, but that was it. It went back to whites only the next night."

"Most of the black groups would come straight to Manteo and perform at Nick's House of Joy, David Latham's or Waders after they played at the Casino," giggled Virginia, "We had a big time."

Her son Michael Tillett added, "The bands would mostly play at Nick's. See, Nick worked some at the Casino, so he would get to know these guys. The players. He would ask them if they want a little side hustle after their gig and they usually did."

Michael also shared that typical juke joint food involved, "a piece of fried fish or fried chicken and a piece of bread. It wasn't much, but it fed the hunger."

"Miss Esther's was where you could always get a full meal," explained Lovey, "That was some good cookin'."

Collards with Cornmeal Dumplings

Recipe contributed by Chef Lovey Selby, as she remembers from Miss Esther's

4–5 pounds collards, washed and cleaned
¼–½ pound salt pork
Water
Pinch of sugar
Cornmeal dumplings

Place collards and as much salt pork as you like in a large pot. Cover with water and sugar and cover pot and simmer for 45–50 minutes. While simmering, make cornmeal dumplings. Drop individual cornmeal dumplings around the side of the pot and simmer for 20 more minutes with the lid off.

Cornmeal Dumplings

⅔ cup fine-ground white cornmeal
⅓ cup plain flour
Pinch of salt
Pinch of sugar
½ cup water or broth from stew

Combine dry ingredients and add just enough water to hold the mixture together. Use enough water to keep them a little on the wet side. Make small flat dumplings to drop into a stew.

CLARA'S

Manteo

The town of Manteo has perfected the art of quaint. The tiny community edging the scenic Shallowbag Bay is rich with history; the street names alone indicate a commitment to legacy and sense of place. Sir Walter Raleigh meets his end at Queen Elizabeth's intersection, and the streets named after them do the same. This is where the Waterfront Shops opened to much fanfare in the mid-1980s.

The complex has one grand restaurant space, and according to local publisher and author Beth Storie, "In 1986 Café Rene opened in the newly constructed Waterfront Shops in downtown Manteo after a successful run in the galleon shops in Nags Head. It closed in 1988, and in 1991 Clara's opened, owned by the famous local restaurant family that operates Owens' Restaurant and [then] RV's."

Donna Hollowell, one of the original owners of the shopping and living development, recalled, "We were thrilled that Café Rene was in the space, the food was delicious. Of course, we loved Clara's, too."

Above: Clara's dining room in the Waterfront Shops in Manteo. *From the private collection of Melody Leckie.*

Right: An advertisement for Clara's in the Waterfront Shops in Manteo. *From the private collection of Melody Leckie.*

The Tradition Continues...

It began in the 1930's and now spans three generations on the Outer Banks. The philosophy was simple...good honest food at good honest prices. The same holds true today as the grand-daughter of Bob and Clara Owens carries on the family tradition on the waterfront in Manteo just down the street from where it all began. Come as you are to Clara's, where the Art Deco Decor suits any mood. There's even a carry-out window for those on the go. Offering an extensive wine list, fresh yogurt and good times. It's everything that a restaurant should be. Relive a family tradition.

clara's seafood grill

Serving Lunch & Dinner Daily
Located on the Waterfront
Downtown Manteo • 473-1727
Open All Year Round

The Waterfront Shops in Manteo. This location has been the home to Café Rene, Clara's, the Trellis and others, and now operates as the deliciously clever and chic Avenue Grille. *Photo by the author.*

Clara and Robert Owens, who opened their namesake restaurant in 1946, are the matriarch and patriarch of a whole lot of food love. Their daughter, Clara Mae Shannon, and her husband, Lionel Shannon, run the restaurant now, with their daughter Peaches Woodard Eckhardt and her husband, Jim. Peaches was in charge of running Clara's on the waterfront in Manteo, with the support of the entire restaurant clan.

On Facebook, Tina Novak Horak shared that she "loved their She Crab Soup and my Husband and I spent many a rainy spring Outer Banks day sitting at the bar by the steamer and indulging in dozens of sweet and salty steamed oysters and frosty mugs of beer. Both priced ridiculously low! We loved Clara's."

Expansive windows lining two sides of the large, open room, allowing for intimate views of small-town marina life. It was the perfect setup for a swanky event, and many others remember special events like wedding receptions and rehearsal dinners. "We loved being their neighbors," wrote Charlotte Jennette Dixon, "my son's rehearsal party was the last event. It was great!

"We had our wedding reception there," remembered Beth Austin Goldsmith, "they did a beautiful job. Oh, what a night!"

After Clara's, the space changed hands a few more times and became, first, the Waterfront Trellis, then, Adrianna's. Today, you can find a clever and tasty menu at Avenue Waterfront Grille.

GREEN DOLPHIN PUB

Manteo

First billed as Fernando's Ale House, the location became home to the Green Dolphin Pub; it is now cleverly remodeled and Ortega'z is the name on the sign.

"I always miss popping over to the Green Dolphin Pub during a big storm. No matter what, a good time was had by all and there was someone to check in with. Right now, I could so go for some of Ginger's lasagna! Mmmmm," sighed Genevieve "Genna" Mizzell Clark, who lived across the street in downtown Manteo.

Ginger is Ginger Tramontano, the owner and operator who fondly recalls that they "filmed a *Matlock* episode at The Green Dolphin Pub and it was quite an experience!" Andy Griffith lived just down the street, in real life, so this clarified the location selection somewhat.

An advertisement for the Green Dolphin Pub extolling the virtues of the tiny pub that produced big stories, including an episode of *Matlock*. *From the private collection of Melody Leckie.*

The entryway to the Green Dolphin Pub was both inviting and intimidating, depending on the stories you heard before you arrived. Once you made it in, the pub was cozy, inviting and friendly. *From the private collection of Melody Leckie.*

Michael Lay, who also lived nearby, recalled on Facebook, "Oh, the she crab soup! Be still my heart! And really perhaps the best bacon cheeseburger on the Outer Banks. I really like Ortegaz, but I sure do miss The Dolphin. Every town needs a dive, and I mean that in the most positive way. Remember the booths with the worn out seats where you could practically rest your chin on the tabletop like a 5-year-old?"

MANTEO MOTEL COFFEE SHOP

Manteo

"I can still go in that place and place where everything was located," said Melody Leckie, an Outer Banks native who worked in many of the local restaurants and now manages a huge collection of memorabilia and ephemera.

"The restaurant/coffee shop is where El Bueno Taco is today. They had a buffet, upstairs only, when *The Lost Colony* was performing," she shared. The entire property has morphed and changed over the years. "Manteo Motel and the Elizabethan Inn," explained Melody:

the motel cottage cottage court was built first and was next to today's Elizabethan. The cottage court was torn down sometime in the 80s or 90s. The Meekins (Ina Evans' parents) and the Evans (Ina and Burwell) ran the motel and later added the Elizabethan Inn (located behind the cottage court) an outdoor pool and made the exterior of the coffee shop look Elizabethan. Even later they added the indoor pool and the extension of more rooms in the 80s I think it was. I worked there in 1975 for a couple of years, as a desk clerk.

In the 1964 *Guide to Dining on the Outer Banks*, the author wrote about the food,

You will find complete a la carte and dinner menu choices—a fine selection of locally caught seafood along with steaks, ham, chicken, pork chops and others. You will enjoy our daily variety of fresh vegetables. And don't hesitate to bring the family; the dinner prices are moderate and the menu choice is wide. You might like to begin your meal with a bowl of extraordinarily good clam chowder.

Manteo Motel Coffee Shop Clam Chowder

¼ pound bacon
1 teaspoon MSG
2 onions, chopped
1 tablespoon salt
1 stalk celery, chopped
1 teaspoon oregano
1 quart minced clams
1 teaspoon white pepper
1 carrot, grated
2 potatoes, diced

Fry out bacon until crisp, crumble. Put bacon and drippings in pot with 6 quarts water. Add all ingredients except potatoes and cook 20 minutes. Add potatoes and cook additional 10 minutes. Thicken with flour.

The guide also advertised, "A special dinner feature during the summer season is our 'Quick Colony Special' for those of you who want to eat well but quickly enough to make the first scene comfortably. A sample menu might be baked Rock Fish (Striped Bass), choice of two vegetables, hush puppies, beverage and dessert, for $1.50."

They even included the recipe.

Baked Rockfish

Cut a large rock into quarters, rub with bacon drippings and place in baking pan. Sprinkle with MSG, salt and pepper. Pour a Spanish sauce (made from tomatoes, green pepper, onion and seasoning) over the fish and bake, basting several times.

The advertised midday meal was described as "For luncheon, we serve daily specials complete with beverage and dessert, for 97 cents. That means a full and delicious lunch for $1.00 including tax. Our local people especially enjoy them all year round."

The current restaurant used to be the casual coffee shop, advertised with "booths, tables, and breakfast bar." The more formal eatery was upstairs in what was called the Roanoke Room where, "Our service allows you to eat hastily or linger over a U.S. Choice Sirloin on a sizzling platter for $2.35."

WALKER'S DINER, THE DUCHESS OF DARE

Manteo

Court cases may or may not have been decided at Walker's Diner and, when remodeled, renamed the Duchess of Dare, but there is a good chance most were heard. The sheriff, the DA, the assistant DA, the judge and various other cohorts regularly met for lunch on Fridays.

Friday was court day, and a small crew of the prosecutorial variety congregated each week to sup on the freshest fish available. They had a standing date, and no one joined their table unless invited.

From *Outer Banks Magazine* in 1989: "The 'Duchess,' Doris Walker, has been serving her 'family' of locals, vacationers and the courthouse crowd

Photographer Drew C. Wilson, who captured the image, shares, "For you folks that aren't familiar with the situation here, I was at the diner doing a story about the place and encountered this crowd at 'the table' when Kenny says he doesn't want his picture taken. Well, before I could say no problem, he climbs up on his seat and steps onto the table. I took his picture then! So he hops down and demands that I give him the film. I refuse and he twists the lens off of the camera and puts it in his pocket. There was quite a scene there for a minute between us. I had asked for the uniformed deputy who was sitting there (who shall go unnamed, not. I think his name was Sam Pledger) and he was no help at all. Finally, the Duchess intervened and got it back. I went straight to the office, developed the film, made a print, and took it back the the Duchess and it was framed behind the table until the place closed. Years later I presented Kenny with an 11x14 of the print and he was very appreciative." According to Linda Crumpler Pearce, on Outer Banks Vintage Scrapbook website, "the people in the photo have been identified as: Kenny Whittington (on the table trying to get out of the picture); and left to right around the table—Merle Meekins, Andy Mihovch (partly covered by Kenny's leg), Saint Basnight Jr. (you can see just the top of his head behind Dave), Dave Austin, and Skip Dixon (standing)." *Photo by Drew C. Wilson, courtesy Outer Banks History Center.*

for more than forty years." The Duchess serves daily specials, including fresh local seafood, and homemade desserts. (Her bread pudding and rice pudding have a loyal following.) The restaurant is right across the street from the Pioneer Movie Theatre, near *Elizabeth II* and the waterfront."

The Duchess of Dare in downtown Manteo was a popular destination for both local gossip and home cooking. The location is now the home to 108 Budleigh, an event space. *Photo by Aycock Brown, courtesy Outer Banks History Center.*

Laura Cuthrell Ward remembers being raised on the fried shrimp, and she recalls all the details of the menu—Ward's aunt was the Duchess herself. As she reminisced, she would add comments such as, "Forgot about the bread pudding."

"They had the best hush puppies!! The cooks would sneak them to me when I was little," Ward also exclaimed.

REEF RESTAURANT

The Causeway

In the battle of lace cornbread, she who prints it, wins it. At least that is what we are going with. Ann Gray and her husband, Dick, were the owners of the Reef Dining Room, on the Nags Head–Manteo causeway, across from the now Oasis Suite and the then Oasis Restaurant. The Oasis also advertised lace cornbread, right on the building.

According to legend, Ann Gray learned the recipe while in Mexico. Similar recipes appeared and continue to appear around the Outer Banks. Some recipes have onions, some do not. Here is the recipe the Grays had printed on a takeaway for their guests, and reviews and promotions repeated the story.

The *Dining Guide to the Outer Banks* shared,

> *Dick and Ann Gray's Reef Dining Room is one of Nags Head's choice seafood restaurants. Every one who over the years, has been devotees of the Reef, already know how delicious their fried shrimp is, and the famous Ann-originated lace cornbread, is a specialty there. The matter of the lace cornbread came about during a trip to Mexico Ann and Dick took some years ago, where Ann watched the Indian women cooking the corn delicacy over an open fire.*
>
> *Now known coast to coast as an accompaniment to seafood, and also for between-meal snacks lace cornbread is just one of the many dining specialties at the Reef. You will also enjoy the Reef's fine broiled steaks, U.S. Choice Delmonico, a 10 ounce steak, also the 6 ounce Delmonico. Fried chicken, broiled crabmeat in butter, fried clams and scallops, and many other good things at the Reef.*

Ann Gray's Lace Cornbread

1 cup white cornmeal
1 ¾ cups water
1 level teaspoon salt
Dash pepper
1 small onion, chopped fine

Mix all ingredients well. Drop from a tablespoon into ¼ inch hot fat, allowing 2 tablespoons batter to a corncake. Brown well and turn to cook on other side, turning only once. Drain on paper towels. Makes about 2 dozen.

OASIS

The Causeway

Violet Kellam's Oasis Seafood Restaurant is one of the most written about restaurants of bygone days. The reason? The barefoot coeds, of course.

Wrote Isabel Murphy in 1964, "In addition to its attractive location, good food and atmosphere, the Oasis employs only College Co-eds as waitresses, working their way through school, who serve in Bermuda Shorts and Bare Feet. For this project, added to many others," she also added, "Mrs. Kellem was awarded the 1962 'Mother of the Year' award." She did not say from whom.

The restaurant property in now home to a lodging establishment, Oasis Suites. The location, on the causeway, was once called Treasure Island.

Added Murphy, "The Oasis is built on man-made land, formerly marshes. The dining room consists of a screened porch overlooking Roanoke Sound, and it resembles an art gallery as the walls are adorned with 25 paintings by one artist, the owner. From a waterside table one may watch boat races, water skiers, diving sea gulls or fishermen on the bridge."

Some tell that Violet Kellam sold the West Soundside Road cottage originally owned by Theodore Miller of Elizabeth City to Ralph and

The Oasis by air. You can see the sign for lacy corncakes—they were that big of a draw. *Photo by Roger Meekins, courtesy Outer Banks History Center.*

"The Original Home of Lace Cornbread." "German Fries and Barefoot College Waitresses" is the message printed on the back of a postcard for the business. The Oasis was known for its barefoot coeds, otherwise known as waitresses, who wore Bermuda shorts and, somehow, no shoes. *Postcard photo by Donna Soyars, Outer Banks Vintage Scrapbook.*

The Oasis dining room. *Photo by Chas D'amours, courtesy Outer Banks History Center.*

The Oasis waterfront restaurant, located on the Manteo–Nags Head causeway. *Photo by Roger Meekins, courtesy Outer Banks History Center.*

Kathryn Oates so that she could finance the purchase of the Oasis restaurant from Dick and Ann Gray, who then built the Reef right across the street.

This is quite a feat. Today, it would be hard to get permits to build on top of a marsh.

Local historian Melody Leckie shared, "This restaurant was purchased by Warren Jones in the 80s and renamed 'The Dock.' Later the original owners family purchased it and renamed it back to the Oasis. Sadly, it was lost to a fire in 2005. Now Oasis Suites is there."

4
Southern Outer Banks

Rodanthe, Waves, Salvo, Avon, Frisco, Buxton, Hatteras

A s you drive south, over Oregon Inlet, you feel like you are entering another dimension. With sand piled high, on both sides of the road in some places, it is hard to fathom that the ocean is just over the east dune and the Pamlico Sound just on the other side of the one to the west.

There is no other road on the Outer Banks that provides the surreality, peacefulness and gratitude inducement as the southern end of Route 12, especially around Pea Island. Windswept and green, or brown and salt covered from a recent storm, the blue sky provides a larger-than-life screen for viewing the clouds, both fluffy and turbulent.

Jeffrey's Seafood fish house in Hatteras Village is one of few remaining fish houses on the Outer Banks. This shot was taken in the afternoon, just after the fishing boats started unloading. *Photo by the author.*

Wax seafood boxes are a sign of prosperity. While a few may make it to local restaurants, the majority will be filled with crushed ice and wild-caught seafood to be shipped to distributors all over the country; a large proportion of that is then shipped internationally. *Photo by the author.*

The villages are dotted along the way; Rodanthe is the first one south of Bonner Bridge, and Hatteras Village is the southernmost, where you will find the ferry docks and an opportunity to continue your journey farther south.

Fishing is a pretty big deal around here, both commercially and recreationally. Restaurant menus reflect the abundance, and locally caught just-fried fish or shrimp are must-have meals when eating your way around the food history of the island.

DOWN UNDER

Rodanthe

Chef Sheila Collie at the Down Under made the best stuffed jalapeño peppers on the island, according to Hatteras Island native Antoinette Mattingly, "Oh, they were so good. She stuffed them with shrimp and cheese and then wrapped them in bacon. Mmmm."

When I asked Sheila about them, she said, "The dish you are referring to was called Down Under Shrimp, and yes, it was very popular." Located on the Rodanthe Pier, "We opened in 1991 and sold in 1999," Sheila shared.

Yes, you can still eat her cooking, now at Sheila's Carolina Kitchen, inside the clubhouse at Cape Hatteras KOA. When the campground rebuilt after flooding a few years back, management added a raised building with a cute little eatery inside; you do not have to be a guest of the KOA to eat there.

Local artist Michael Halminski wrote in 2017,

> *Over the years I've seen restaurants here come and go. Some fail faster than others, and it's not an easy business to achieve success. It's about quality, quantity and customer satisfaction, among other things.*
>
> *One of the most successful restaurants in our town was started at a location where several other restaurants had come and gone. The Rodanthe pier complex had reincarnations of restaurants in the same building with names like Cross Currents, Under Currents, and JL Seagull. There were others prior whose names have escaped me.*
>
> *Undoubtedly the most successful was the Down Under founded by Skip and Sheila Skiperdene. The name was coined by Australian ex-pat surfer Skip, who married Sheila, a North Carolinian, and they began the Aussie-*

The Rodanthe Pier, the original home of the Down Under Restaurant, loses a little bit more of itself with each storm, but as of 2019, it was still operating as a fishing and sightseeing pier with a small bait and retail shop. *Photo by the author.*

themed restaurant. It took a year or so to catch on, but with planning and hospitality it became hugely popular. Most summer evenings had dozens of patrons lined up outside the front door waiting to be seated. This went on for about ten years, when personal circumstances ended the epic run of Down Under circa 1999.

The proximity to the ocean made a dramatic venue for diners but also contributed to its demise.

An aspiring restaurateur then bought the trademarked name and stepped in to continue to operate the business. Something, however, was missing, and the restaurant was not quite the same. A few years later, things really went south when Hurricane Isabel pummeled the property.

CAPTAIN'S TABLE

Frisco

Outdoor port and starboard lights and seashore-inspired dining room décor created a seagoing atmosphere for island diners. Semiprivate dining rooms held small groupings of tables, and the restaurant also offered dining in one of several small private dining rooms.

George Fuller's Captain's Table Restaurant on Hatteras Island, was located in Frisco, between Buxton and Hatteras Village, and it specialized in "Seafood Cape Hatteras Style, and Sizzling Steaks." In an ad from the mid-1960s, Fuller was quoted:

They serve the very best food obtainable, prepared according to Hatteras recipes and up-to-date know-how. For instance, we are featuring a Captain's deluxe seafood combination dinner, containing just about every variety of seafood fresh from the ocean. Also a real old Cape Hatteras clam chowder that wins applause too. As for the Captain's Table steaks, they're extra fine, thick, juicy and broiled to perfection.

Fuller credited Mrs. Cecil (Zilphia) Austin of Hatteras Village as "the ship's wheel in the galley, who will see to it that your food is to your liking."

There is another restaurant also named Captain's Table, in the former Captain Dave's location, but it is not the same as the one described.

The current Quarterdeck Restaurant was the former site of George Fuller's Captain's Table. Before that, it was Tandy's, a dance hall or juke joint. *Photo by the author.*

Deviled Crabs

1 pound crab meat
1 cup breadcrumbs, toasted
½ stick butter, melted
1 egg
½ cup grated cheese
1 teaspoon prepared mustard
1 tablespoon chopped parsley
2 teaspoons lemon juice
1 tablespoon Worcestershire sauce
Pinch dry mustard

Mix all together and put in crab shells. Add more bread crumbs, dot with butter and grated cheese. Bake 30 minutes in a moderate oven.

Hatteras Cake

1 pound raisins
2 cups flour
1 ½ cups sugar
2 teaspoons cinnamon
1 teaspoon nutmeg
1 teaspoon baking soda
1 teaspoon salt
2 eggs, beaten
½ cup shortening, melted
½ cup applesauce

Cover raisins with water and boil about 20 minutes. Sift together dry ingredients, add raisins and mix with water from raisins. Add beaten eggs, applesauce and melted shortening and pour batter into baking pan and bake at 350 about 45 minutes.

SCOTTIE'S RESTAURANT

Hatteras

Scottie's Restaurant was located next to the Atlantic View Hotel in Hatteras Village and had an outstanding reputation for fresh local seafood and hearty breakfasts. W. Scottie and Nettie Gibson were the original owners and operators, and then they passed the torch to Ray and Dora Long, who continued the the Hatteras-style menu.

The guests of both the hotel and the restaurant were primarily fishermen, and they were fed hearty meals before embarking, or after finishing, a day of surf, inlet or Gulf Stream fishing.

A recently found breakfast menu featured an "Old Fashioned" breakfast with choice of cereal, two eggs (as you like them), buttered toast and jelly and hot coffee, all for seventy-five cents.

According to an article from the mid-1960s, Scottie's also specialized

in fresh-from-the-seafood, home-made soups and a real special clam chowder, crabmeat in butter, shrimp as you like them, native scallops, crabs, soft shell and crabmeat cakes and fresh-caught fish broiled to your liking. Meats include a fine roast beef, prime ribs in natural gravy, steaks and fried chicken. Clams on the half shell, and fried oysters, broiled lobster tails, are also on the menu at Scottie's. Home-made cornbread, hush puppies and rolls, as home-made pies are included.

Crabmeat Cakes

9 slices bread, diced
1 can evaporated milk
3 pounds crab meat
6 tablespoons prepared mustard
2 eggs
2 teaspoons salt
1 teaspoon pepper

Soak bread in milk, mix with other ingredients and shape into cakes. Fry in hot fat, about ½ inch in skillet, brown on one side and turn.

CHANNEL BASS

Hatteras

In 2003, Channel Bass restaurant became a casualty of Hurricane Isabel. The storm wreaked havoc on Hatteras Island and even cut a new inlet, isolating the island from the northern beaches for several months. The restaurant persevered, though, and rebuilt, changing hands a couple of times before being torn down in 2017.

The last few years might have been rough, but the Channel Bass will always be remembered as an iconic family eatery and one of the first restaurants in Hatteras Village.

Local historian and island native Danny Couch fondly remembered the Harrison family, who owned the restaurant for almost forty years: "They served seafood straight from the boats."

In September 2017, the local news source, the *Island Free Press*, reported that the former Channel Bass Restaurant in Hatteras Village was torn down.

CHANNEL BASS RESTAURANT

SEAFOOD—"Direct From Ocean To You"

WE PREPARE LUNCHES FOR HUNTING AND FISHING TRIPS

or

"Take-Out" Orders To Go

Open Year-Round—5:00 A.M.-10:00 P.M.
Evelyn Styron, Manager
Bob and Marion Ballance, Owners

PHONE: 995-2921

Write: P. O. Box 124

HATTERAS, N. C.

An advertisement for Channel Bass, in Hatteras Village. *From the private collection of Melody Leckie.*

Joy Crist wrote that "longtime visitors to Hatteras village may notice a local landmark missing on their next trip to the southern end of the island—namely, the former Channel Bass restaurant. Originally opened in the late 1950s, the Channel Bass was one of the first restaurants in Hatteras village, and was established even before the Bonner Bridge and a fully paved Highway 12 was added to the island landscape."

Jackie Harrison, who owned the restaurant for nearly forty years with his wife, Shelby, and two daughters, Brenda and Debbie, was quoted as saying he wasn't too sad about the structure's removal. "I've known about it for about six months, so I'm not too surprised," said Jackie. "I'm actually glad to see it being torn down, because in the last 4–5 years, it got to be an eyesore."

The Channel Bass opened around 1958, and Jackie and his family bought the restaurant in 1965. For decades, the Channel Bass served only seafood that was caught by local anglers. "Most of the fish came right off the boats," said Jackie's daughter Debbie. "It was nothing but Hatteras style seafood, and the food was impeccable. [Fishermen] would come into the village marinas, get fish in the cooler, and then bring it right to our back door."

At the time, Jackie estimated that there were four restaurants in the area—which includes Sonny's and the Quarterdeck—and the Channel Bass was already an established eatery for the handful of visitors who made the trek south in the wintertime.

In 1964, just before the Harrisons bought the restaurant, Isabel Murphy wrote,

The Channel Bass is under the expert management of Mrs. Evelyn Styron whose more than 12 years experience in food preparation and serving is evidenced by the excellent food served at the Channel Bass. When dining there be sure to order their Hatteras style clam chowder, it's the old-fashion kind and is really tops. I'm sure you'll call for more. Their seafood is served fresh from Hatteras waters, and their steaks, fried chicken and other good things to eat, are dining treats. For dessert, Evelyn's pies are food for the gods and are baked fresh every morning and even better than the pies "mother used to make."

A window table on the waterside is first choice for watching water traffic on the Slash and for a relaxing view of the meandering creek, while enjoying breakfast, lunch or dinner at the Channel Bass. The Channel Bass also prepares box lunches and orders to take out.

The Harrisons kept the name Channel Bass after they bought it, and though it was a quick sale, the restaurant was not necessarily an overnight success. With a sparse visitor population, Jackie estimates that in the first couple of years, the family made about $6,000 annually.

"The first year, we tried opening in winter. The second year, we did the same thing, and we found that it was a disaster," says Jackie. "So after the first couple of years, we quit opening in the off season."

The folks at Divehatteras.com remember the last years: "This icon of Hatteras eateries was sold in '06 and renamed to 'Captain Jacks' but then closed in the first season, and came back again with the original name! However, after just one season it is now closed again and for sale. It was Teach's Bar and Grill for a short time and now it is gone for good as the building was demolished in 2017."

AUSTIN CREEK GRILL

Hatteras

Austin Creek Grill at Hatteras Landing, next to the ferry dock, was a hangout for both locals and celebrities. Serving contemporary Carolina seafood and Southern specialties, the waterfront bistro was a favorite from the minute the doors opened in 1999 until they closed in 2005.

According to Hatteras historian Danny Couch, "Michelle Pfeiffer and her sister, Deedee, were spotted there, on many occasions, as well as sports stars and well known musicians."

The location was lovely, but it was the food that held its own to the same high celebrity standards. Owner and executive chef Ed Daggers was the reason why. A graduate of the Culinary Institute of America and the recipient of numerous awards and accolades within the industry, he brought sophistication, global ingredients and a certain panache to Hatteras Village.

Chef Ed Daggers operated Austin Creek Grill out of this marina location in Hatteras Landing, next to the ferry dock in Hatteras Village. *Photo by the author.*

Both Lauren Ball and Shelby Kinnaird were fortunate to have Chef Ed cater their wedding parties. Said Ball,

> *My husband and I had our wedding back on October 1st of 2005. The reception was held at our favorite Hatteras restaurant, Austin Creek Grill. Several guests commented that it was hands down the best food they had ever had at a wedding reception. I still wish I could go back and have that wasabi encrusted tuna. My mouth waters just thinking about it.*
>
> *One of our favorite appetizers there were the calamari, but I can't remember for sure if that was on the wedding menu. Austin Creek also catered our rehearsal at my in-law's sound front house. Also great food in more of a bbq style with crab balls and cornbread. They even crafted the groom's cake in the shape of a wave!*

When Shelby was asked about her menu, she suggested Rick, her husband, took pretty good notes. She wasn't kidding. He had their whole menu, and wrote a review about the place!

RESTAURANT REVIEW: Austin Creek Grill
The swankiest place on the island
by Rick Kinnaird

Austin Creek Grill is located at the southern tip of Hatteras Island; it's in the shopping center to the right of where you catch the ferry to Ocracoke. It's the most expensive restaurant on the island and has fantastic food. You'd think such a place wouldn't do well on Hatteras, but it's been packed every time we've been there. We suggest you make a reservation if you want to go.

There are actually three parts to Austin Creek: the restaurant, the bakery (Austin Creek Baking Company) and the catering business. They catered our wedding reception in June 2004 and got rave reviews from our guests for both food and service.

They can be, like a lot of folks on Hatteras, devilishly hard to reach by telephone. Don't be discouraged. They will call you back eventually and they will do a good job with your event.

Here's what they served buffet-style at our rehearsal dinner, just to give you a feel for their menu:
Crab Salad on Belgian Endive Leaves
Tomato Basil Bruschetta
Andouille Sausage in Puff Pastry
Austin Creek Spinach Salad—Baby Spinach, Crisp Apples, Poached Pears, Caramelized Pecans, Red Onion & Warm Bacon Dressing
Char-grilled NY Strip au Poivre
Crab Stuffed Flounder with Chili Béarnaise

How was the food? Well, my father-in-law put it best when he said, "I think that was the best steak I've ever had."

We've also eaten at the restaurant a few times and it's fabulous too. One New Year's Eve we were having trouble finding somewhere to go. Austin Creek Grill had two dinner seatings that evening and we managed to snag a last-minute table for a truly memorable night out.

Lemoncello Scampi Shrimp
Serves 4

3–4 jumbo shrimp U-10s Per Person
¼ cup olive oil
1 tablespoon minced shallot
2 tablespoons thin sliced garlic
2 tablespoons chiffonade basil
1 tablespoon lemon zest
1 cup Lemoncello
½ cup white wine
¼ cup fresh squeezed lemon juice
3 tablespoons chopped parsley
3 tablespoons butter, cold cut in small pieces
8 ounces fresh baby arugula
Italian flat leaf parsley for garnish

Peel and de-vein shrimp, rinse and set aside. In heavy sauté pan, heat olive oil until very hot—sauté shrimp in small batches until just cooked through and remove with slotted spoon. Do not overcook!

When shrimp are cooked, add shallot, garlic, basil and half of lemon zest and sauté, being careful not to overcook garlic.

Deglaze with lemoncello and ignite flame to cook off alcohol. Reduce by ¼. Add white wine and lemon juice, reduce again by half.

Add fresh chopped parsley; add shrimp back in to pan and pieces of whole butter until sauce thickens slightly. In serving bowls place small (2-ounce) mounds of baby arugula, spoon shrimp and broth over arugula, garnish with fresh parsley sprig and lemon zest.

5

Ocracoke Island, Hyde County

The only way to access Ocracoke Island is by boat or by plane. The majority of visitors choose a boat, which usually means a ferry. In 2018, the North Carolina Department of Transportation introduced a new passenger ferry to the island. Previously, all the ferries held passengers and their cars. The new all-pedestrian ferry system was highly anticipated, and a shuttle is available to carry passengers from the ferry docks to the village.

Most people don't use their cars when they get to the island anyway. Golf carts now fill the tiny roads and historic streets. Bicyclists and pedestrians round out the mix. Remote Ocracoke Island is twenty-five miles from the mainland and is home to flora and fauna that thrive in the salty coastal environment.

Silver Lake Harbor sits in the middle of the village and provides safe harbor from storms. Ocracoke Island was also the final home of Blackbeard the pirate, and visitors adore the macabre legends.

The year-round population is small, about one thousand people, but the population swells exponentially in the summer. A haven for families and naturalists, season usually begins somewhere around Memorial Day and ends in October with a weekend-long Pirate's Jamboree. This was the final resting place of Blackbeard, after all.

Passenger ferries are the newest addition to the North Carolina fleet. This ferry holds both people and their cars. *Photo by the author.*

WAHAB'S AND THE ISLAND INN

Ocracoke

The Island Inn was Ocracoke's first hotel, and the busy dining room was cozy and comfortable. Located in the heart of the village, the property has had several owners, some more memorable than others. The menu was always Ocracoke-centric, no matter the owners.

According to the Ocracoke Preservation Association, the original purpose of the building was a meeting hall for a group of local men who called themselves the Odd Fellows. Known as the Odd Fellows Lodge, the property was eventually bought by Robert Stanley Wahab Sr., who was born on Ocracoke Island in 1888 to Hatton and Martha Howard Wahab.

Ocracoke Island Inn, pre-demolition. *Photo by the author.*

An abstract from the Outer Banks History Center added,

> *As an adult, after tours at sea, business college, and positions in retail*
> *businesses, education and accounting, Wahab and an associate formed the*
> *company Retail Store Services in 1927, a furniture buying cooperative*
> *for high-end furniture stores that had limited buying power alone. While*
> *running that business until 1947, he built the Wahab Village Hotel in*
> *1936, Ocracoke's first modern hostelry. The Wahab Village expanded to*
> *become a resort including a campground, hunting and fishing club, rental*
> *cottages, and a dinner and dancing club, the "Spanish Casino." Wahab also*
> *helped bring electrical and ice plants, telephone service and improvements to*
> *roads and the ferry service to Ocracoke.*

From the 1964 *Dining on the Outer Banks* guide, "You will enjoy your meals at the Island Inn. They feature Ocracoke style seafoods and an appetizing choice of meats and fresh-baked pies and breads with many other good things to eat."

Left: Wahab's Coffee House was one of the first iterations of eateries in this building. *Right*: The next generation of Ocracoke Island Inn. *Courtesy of Ocracoke Preservation Association.*

At that time, the the Island Inn was owned operated by Mr. and Mrs. Doward Brugh, who boasted of "26 air conditioned rooms with private and connecting baths." This was a big deal on Ocracoke. Ocracoke Island was, and is still, accessible only by ferry from Hatteras Island or the ferry from Cedar Island and the mainland.

Home-style meals were fare of the day in the mid-1960s and appeared to be similar in the 1980s. The recipes found were published when the inn was owned by Ocracoke native Larry Williams. He shared them with author Dawn O'Brien when she visited in the early 1980s. They are featured in her book *North Carolina's Historic Restaurants and Their Recipes.*

The following She Crab Soup with Marigold is a curious and clever recipe. Using readily available ingredients, such as a can of cream of celery soup, the clever cook uses the marigold to replace the color that is normally imparted with golden orange eggs from female crabs, the roe—it is noticeably absent in the list of ingredients. Purists scoff when there are no eggs in she crab soup; it is not she crab soup. Period.

She Crab Soup with Marigold

2 cans cream of celery soup
3 cups milk
1 cup half-and-half
2 boiled eggs, chopped

½ cup butter or margarine
½ teaspoon Old Bay seasoning
½ teaspoon Worcestershire sauce
¼ teaspoon garlic salt
¼ teaspoon white pepper
1 cup crab meat, drained and flaked
¼ cup dry sherry
Chopped marigold leaves

Combine soup, milk, cream, eggs, butter, Old Bay, Worcestershire, garlic and pepper in a large Dutch oven; bring to a boil. Add crab meat and cook over medium heat, stirring occasionally until heated through. Stir in sherry. Sprinkle each serving with marigold leaves. Yields about 2 quarts.

Ocracoke Island Inn, the restaurant side, pre-demolition. *Photo by the author.*

Island Inn's Kiss

½ ounce Galliano
1 scoop vanilla ice cream
Colored sugar crystals

In a champagne glass, place ¼ ounce Galliano. Add ice cream. Pour another ¼ ounce Galliano over ice cream. Sprinkle with colored sugar crystals. Keep at room temperature until ice cream begins to melt. Place in freezer until ready to serve. Serves 1.

CAFÉ ATLANTIC

Ocracoke Island

The first time Ruth Toth ever saw a whole tuna loin, it was on the prep table at a restaurant she worked at in Buxton in the mid-1970s. She asked the owner what he was going to do with the big red slab of meat. His response, said Ruth, was that it had been given to him and the only thing that could be done to it was boil it and can it.

Since then, Ruth said she couldn't begin to estimate how much tuna they have sold or how many different ways they prepared it.

The Toths were innovative before they knew it. Ruth also noted that "we were the first restaurant on Ocracoke to serve grilled seafood. That was in 1989," she giggled, "another trend I didn't know we were in the middle of."

Ruth and her husband, Bob, often found themselves in the middle of things before they knew what happened. The restaurant, Café Atlantic, might even be one of those things.

"We decided to build the restaurant and it was totally irrational," said Ruth. "I had some experience and Bob had none, but, he could fix anything. All he asked was to not make him cook."

"Well, at the time, I was still teaching full time, so we hired a chef," continued Ruth, "it wasn't long before the chef had a family illness and Bob was trained. He has been cooking ever since."

Introducing new species of fish was always a risk, but their clientele was adventurous. "One day a young man came by with some fresh fish. We asked him what he had and he said triggerfish. We said sure and he

Ruth Toth holds a copy of her cookbook *Café Atlantic*, featuring recipes from the restaurant. A few of them are reprinted here. *Photo by Peter Vankovich.*

Just-caught tuna, pan-seared, on the rare side, has been a popular dish on many local menus since the early 1990s. *Photo by the author.*

looked up, kinda startled, and said 'you do?' Once the staff tasted it, they pushed it; you only have to taste it once."

In October 2013, Jenny Scarborough wrote in the *Ocracoke Current*, "The Cafe Atlantic will close forever after four more dinner services. Customers are sad. Owners Bob and Ruth Toth are happy. They want to take a vacation together, in the summer. Alaska! That has not been possible for them for the 25 years they have owned, managed and worked in their restaurant, which opened in the spring of 1989."

"Saying goodbye to the café is bittersweet," shared Scarborough, who was also a part-time waitress, "like the chocolate cream pie."

The café also was the first island restaurant to serve brunch. Ruth said that "lunchtime on Sundays were slow. The first brunches 'maybe 35 to 50' people were served. Then we started to get regulars." People wanted her huevos rancheros, the lemon ricotta pancakes and the shrimp and grits.

The dining room was described in the 1999 issue of *Outer Banks Magazine*:

> *Ruth and Bob Toth cordially invite you to dine with them at Cafe Atlantic. The two story restaurant sports a pickled wood interior and a large expanse of glass that provides diners with an excellent view of the surrounding dunes and marsh. Grilled, baked and sautéed fish and shellfish star here. Crab cakes, vegetarian entrées and our grilled seafood platter are customer favorites. All desserts are homemade. Our Sunday Brunch is a favorite with the locals.*

Everything was a favorite.

Falafel

"This was a very popular sandwich at lunch," Toth wrote in her cookbook. "We served four falafel balls in whole wheat pit halves garnished with lettuce, tomatoes, onions, sprouts and the customer's choice of dressing."

2 cups canned chickpeas, drained and rinsed
1 teaspoon minced garlic
¼ cup chopped celery
¼ cup chopped scallions
¼ teaspoon cumin
¼ teaspoon coriander
⅛ teaspoon cayenne

⅛ teaspoon black pepper
¾ teaspoon salt
I egg
2 tablespoons tahini
3 tablespoons flour
Oil for frying

Add half of the chickpeas to food processor work bowl. Add all other ingredients and process. Add rest of the peas and process until well blended. To cook: drop heaping tablespoon of batter into hot oil (350) and cook until it is browned.

Pickled Shrimp/Caribbean Shrimp Cocktail

Ocracoke trendsetter, perpetual beacon of good taste and Zillie's Island Pantry owner David Bundy shared this recipe for pickled shrimp with owner Ruth Toth, and it became a perennial favorite at Café Atlantic. Toth proclaims it to be the best shrimp cocktail she ever ate; she called it Caribbean Shrimp Cocktail on her menu.

30 large shrimp, peeled, deveined and tails removed.
½ cup thinly sliced purple onion
3 navel oranges, peeled and sectioned
2 tablespoons capers
½ medium red pepper, cut into thin strips
2 tablespoons chopped cilantro

Marinade

½ cup white wine vinegar
2 tablespoons ketchup
5 tablespoons canola oil
¼ cup fresh lemon juice
½ teaspoon celery salt
½ teaspoon minced garlic
¼ teaspoon ground black pepper
I teaspoon salt
I teaspoon mustard seed
⅛ teaspoon cayenne

Boil shrimp until just barely done. Chill in an ice bath. While the shrimp are chilling, prep the remaining ingredients. and place in a medium large bowl. Drain shrimp well, whisk together marinade ingredients in a small bowl. Pour marinade over shrimp and toss gently to disperse marinade. Marinate overnight. Just before serving, add chopped avocado or place wedge of avocado in each serving. Makes 6 portions.

Lime and Ginger Pots De Creme

2 teaspoons lime zest
⅔ cup freshly squeezed lime juice
1 tablespoon minced fresh ginger
1 cup sugar
8 eggs
1 cup half-and-half

Preheat oven to 325. Whisk all ingredients together and fill 6-ounce oven-proof custard cups ¾ full. Bake in hot water bath about 40 minutes or until center is only slightly liquid. Yields 7 servings.

Baked Fish with Creamy Lemon Dill Sauce

"This is good with any local fish," wrote Ruth, "and it is also a terrific way to fix salmon."

1 ½ cups mayonnaise
⅓ cup sour cream
⅓ cup fresh chopped dill or 2 tablespoons dried dill
1 tablespoon Grey Poupon mustard
1 teaspoon garlic
Zest and juice from one lemon
Paprika, to taste

Mix all ingredients well. Spread fish filet with topping before baking. Sprinkle with paprika. Bake in a 425-degree oven until cooked through. Time will depend on the thickness of the filet, but typically takes about 15 minutes.

Tuna Marinade

One of the most popular entrées on Ruth and Bob Toth's menu at Café Atlantic on Ocracoke Island was the grilled tuna. This is the marinade recipe.

⅓ cup brown sugar
1 ½ cups soy sauce
1 cup water
1 tablespoon fresh grated ginger
2 teaspoons minced garlic
½ teaspoon black pepper
½ teaspoon hot sauce
1 ½ cups white wine

In a medium bowl, whisk ingredients together until the sugar dissolves.

Ruth notes: We don't marinate the tuna until after it is ordered. Leave the tuna in the marinade about 5 minutes and cook over a medium–hot grill. Use the sauce to baste the fish as it cooks. You can also serve the marinade on the side as a dipping sauce with wasabi paste.

Ocracoke Fig Cake

The Toths served this traditional moist spice cake with a scoop of coffee ice cream. Try it!

3 eggs
1 ½ cups sugar
1 cup oil
2 cup flour
1 teaspoon baking soda
1 teaspoon salt
1 teaspoon cinnamon
1 teaspoon nutmeg
1 teaspoon allspice
½ cup buttermilk
1 teaspoon vanilla
1 ½ cups preserved figs, drained and coarsely chopped
1 cup walnuts or pecans

Preheat oven to 350 degrees. Beat eggs, add sugar and oil. Sift flour and other dry ingredients. Add to egg mix alternately with buttermilk and vanilla. Fold in figs and nuts. Bake approximately 1 hour for a tube pan, a little less for a 13 x 9 pan. Yields 12 servings.

Fig Preserves
By Myra E. Wahab

Use only well-ripened figs, peel carefully and put in kettle to be used for cooking. Weigh kettle first to be sure of accurate weight of fruit used. Cooking in small amounts, I prefer 6 pounds at a time, gives a more pleasing preserve.

6 pounds figs, peeled
3 pounds sugar
2 medium lemons, thinly sliced and seeded

Pour sugar gradually over figs—this lets it settle in kettle. Do not stir. Add lemon on top of sugar. Start with a moderate heat; tip kettle from time to time to be sure syrup is forming. When all sugar is thoroughly wet with syrup, increase heat and bring to steady boil, not a roping boil. Carefully stir occasionally to keep from breaking figs. Cook until the syrup is ropey, not too thick, but like a good syrup. Pour immediately into sterilized jars and seal.

Figs grow all over Ocracoke Island, and preserves are put up by all sorts of good folks. You can find jars available from a few local online retailers.

THE PELICAN

Ocracoke

When Debbie Wells moved to Ocracoke, she created a brand-new food scene all by herself. Well, it does take an island, so, maybe not all by herself, but close. She was the chef and a founder of both the Pelican and the Back Porch Restaurants, two of Ocracoke's most iconic eateries. She is still on the scene, creating and making. Her fig preserves are available in local markets.

Wells brought new ingredients to the island at a time when fried was the only option available for seafood, unless it was boiled or cooked outside on a fire—not a fire meaning a grill, but a fire meaning an outdoor pit fire. The fish were impaled on long sticks that were stuck into the ground at an angle so the fish could roast over the open flame. Just-caught mullet was a favorite fish to cook this way.

As if visiting the future, Phyllis C. Richman wrote in a 1985 column featured in the *Washington Post,*

> *The restaurant anthropologists could have a field day on Ocracoke Island in North Carolina. They could aim their notebooks at the 10 little eateries and watch them grow and change with the times, for they are just at the beginning.*
>
> *Only a few hundred people live year-round on the island, but in the summer the population swells to more than 3,000, estimate the locals. And there isn't much to do but sun and eat. In fact, until this decade there wasn't much of the latter, either. You could have "island seafood," which meant fried stuff. And that was about it.*
>
> *Then eight years ago Debbie Wells came to Ocracoke from Atlanta—just for the summer. She stayed on, however, and dreamed of opening a restaurant, having worked in kitchens in Atlanta for years and discovered a "big gap" in Ocracoke. Along the way she married John Wells, who had been a food service manager for Johns Hopkins University and chain restaurants, and together they undertook to manage a new restaurant—The Pelican—for four years until they were ready to start their own. In February 1984 the Wells opened their own restaurant, the Back Porch, which the locals now refer to as "the gourmet restaurant," the one that caters to "city tastes." It even has a vegetarian entrée, which goes over well particularly with tourists, say the staff. A vegetarian entrée. Imagine that.*

An expert with ingredients, Wells would introduce a new twist to familiar ingredients. Her crab beignets are a great example. Still fried, still using local seafood, the beignets were just oh, so sophisticated.

Crab Beignets

Makes about 16

Filling

1 pound claw meat of blue crab, cooked and picked
1 pound cream cheese
1 ½ teaspoons tarragon leaves
2 tablespoons Worcestershire sauce
1 teaspoon chopped garlic

Crêpes

1 cup flour
⅔ cup milk
⅔ cup water
3 eggs
¼ teaspoon salt
3 tablespoons butter, melted

Batter

1 cup flour
2 tablespoons cornstarch
1 teaspoon baking powder
½ teaspoon salt
2 whole eggs
1 egg yolk
1 tablespoon soy oil
½ to ¾ cup water
Lettuce for serving
Lemon wedges for serving
Dijon mustard for serving

Mix filling ingredients. Set aside. Mix crêpe ingredients and let sit for 1 hour. Heat a small crêpe pan until smoking. Brush lightly with oil. Make crêpes by swirling 1 ounce of batter over the surface of a small (6-inch) crêpe pan. Cook until crisp around the edges and turn once, cooking until done. Continue until all the batter is used.

When crêpes are finished, place 2 ounces of filling in each crêpe. Roll up crêpe and tuck the ends under. (They may be refrigerated at this point for up to 12 hours.)

To make the batter, mix dry ingredients together. Mix wet ingredients together and then fold the 2 mixtures gently together. Dip crêpes in batter. Put oil in a pot until it reaches 2 to 3 inches. Fry crêpes in oil until brown on both sides, turning once. Serve immediately on lettuce with lemon wedges and mustard.

Marinated Vegetables

Vegetables

12 green beans
2 medium zucchini, sliced
2 stalks broccoli, cut up and stems removed

Dressing

⅔ cup salad oil
½ cup chopped pimiento
⅓ cup red wine vinegar
1 tablespoon capes
1 tablespoon Grey Poupon mustard
½ cup chopped scallions
¼ teaspoon each: rosemary, thyme, granulated garlic, paprika, dry mustard, honey, salt and cayenne

Steam vegetables separately until crunchy and bright green. Cool. For dressing, stir all ingredients together until well blended. Pour over vegetables. Toss and chill 1 hour or longer. Serves 4–6.

Zucchini, Sour Cream and Dill

4 medium zucchini
3 tablespoons butter

Sauce

3 tablespoons sour cream
2 tablespoons Parmesan cheese
1 tablespoon dill weed
½ teaspoon salt
Dash of granulated garlic

Slice zucchini. Sauté in butter until bright green. Remove and place in a bowl. Combine ingredients for sauce and pour over sautéed zucchini. Serve at once. Serves 4–6.

Conclusion

I hope you had as much fun reading about these jewels as I did researching. Over the course of a year, more material amassed than I could print in one book, so, there had to be a way to narrow down the field.

These lost restaurants made the final cut because they met at least two of the three criteria developed for inclusion: 1) They were beloved and no longer operating; 2) a high-resolution photograph related to the location was found, or taken, within the time frame I had to research and write the book; 3) a recipe was contributed that could be directly sourced to the lost restaurant.

This was my process, and the results are in your hands. The remaining material is the seeding of my next book, *Lost Restaurants of the Outer Banks and Their Recipes*, volume 2.

Stay tuned and stay salty!

Resources

The collections of Outer Banks History Center, North Carolina Department of Archives and Eastern Albemarle Regional Library System, especially their collections of vintage cookbooks and magazines.

Articles

Angione, Kathy. "The Freedmen of Roanoke Island: The Other Lost Colony." SeaGrant North Carolina *Coastwatch* (Holiday 2005). https://ncseagrant.ncsu.edu/coastwatch/previous-issues/2005-2/holiday-2005/the-freedmen-of-roanoke-island-the-other-lost-colony.

Blum, Liz. "Less Time Cooking, Means More Time for Having Fun." Beachcomber, April, 5, 1985, http://www.lizbrummond.com/Documents/OBX-Current-PrintArticle-beachcomber-lesstimemorefun.pdf.

Boldaji, Amelia. "Celebrating the Classics: Kelly's Restaurant, Mako Mike's, Pamlico Jack's, Port O' Call." Outer Banks This Week. July 9, 2014. https://outerbanksthisweek.com/articles/celebrating-classics.

Fox, Larry. "Newer but Still Older." *Washington Post*, August 26, 1988. https://www.washingtonpost.com/archive/lifestyle/1988/08/26/newer-but-still-outer/326841cb-fba0-4a02-83f6-921ed528b859/?utm_term=.28eb410bc94b.

Kozak, Catherine. "To Everything There Is a Seasoning." *Virginian-Pilot*, April 5, 2006. https://pilotonline.com/news/article_e9ec4c4d-aeeb-5fff-9eaf-629d4f12ff5d.html.

Richman, Phyllis C. "Richman's Table." *Washington Post*, September 18, 1985. https://www.washingtonpost.com/archive/lifestyle/food/1985/09/18/richmans-table/d4ed8f3a-cf0f-4d0c-80fa-9018d969f749/?utm_term=.af9df2c2722b.

Storie, Beth P. "A Bite-Size History of Outer Banks Restaurants." Outer Banks This Week. March 27, 2015. https://outerbanksthisweek.com/articles/bite-size-history-outer-banks-restaurants.

Wagner, Michelle. "Port O'Call Has New Owners, New Mission." *Outer Banks Sentinel*, May 1, 2018. https://www.obsentinel.com/news/fresh-start-for-a-storied-venue/article_22cc2684-4d57-11e8-a788-6fda9858fc27.html.

Wells, Pete. "The Simone on the Upper East Side." *New York Times*, June 3, 2014. https://www.nytimes.com/.../restaurant-review-the-simone-on-the-upper-east-side.html.

Books

Beranbaum, Rose Levy. *The Cake Bible*. 8th ed. New York: William Morrow, 1988.

Britthaven of the Outer Banks Residents' Council. *Britthaven Breaks Bread*. Kearney, NE: Morris Press, 1992.

The Chef and The Child Foundation. *Carolina Coastal Chefs, Concoctions: A Gathering of Unique Recipes from the Outer Banks' Favorite Chefs and Restaurateurs*. N.p., 1989.

Click, Patrica. *Time Full of Trial: The Roanoke Island Freedmen's Colony 1862–1867*. Chapel Hill: University of North Carolina Press, 2001.

Downing, Sarah. *Vintage Outer Banks: Shifting Sands and Bygone Beaches*. Charleston, SC: The History Press, 2008.

Ehringhaus, Ann Sebrell. *Ocracoke Portrait, Photography and Interviews*. Winston-Salem, NC: John F. Blair, 1988.

Harrison, Molly Perkins. *It Happened on the Outer Banks*. Guilford, CT: TwoDot, 2005.

Johnson, Henry Vanderbilt. *Kronicles of a Kolored Kid*. CreateSpace, 2012.

Murphy, Isabel. *A Guide to Dining on the Outer Banks*. N.p., 1964.

O'Brien, Dawn. *North Carolina's Historic Restaurants and Their Recipes*. Winston-Salem, NC: John F. Blair, 1983.

Outer Banks Woman's Club. *A Book of Favorite Recipes*. Kill Devil Hills, NC: self-published, 1968–1986.

Toth, Ruth Goins. *Café Atlantic Cook Book*. 2nd ed. N.p.: self-published, 2015.

United Methodist Church of Ocracoke. *Ocracoke Cook Book*. Ocracoke Island, NC: self-published, 1990.

Wiegand, Elizabeth. *The Outer Banks Cookbook*. Guilford, CT: ThreeForks, 2008.

Publications/Websites

Ancestry.com
Coastland Times
Facebook.com
Findagrave.com
Insider's Guide to the Outer Banks
Island Free Press
New York Times
Outer Banks Explorer
Outer Banks magazine, the vintage version.
Outer Banks Sentinel
Outer Banks Voice
Sunny Day
Virginian-Pilot
Washington Post

Other

Outer Banks Taste of the Beach 2013 brochure. http://www.obxtasteofthebeach.com/documents/Program-pages-2013-forweb_001.pdf.

Recipe Index

Soups and Chowders

For Sharing

Entrées

Index

About the Author

Naturally curious, Amy Pollard Gaw is a reformed restaurateur, feeder, writer, educator and collector of food lore who enjoys helping others find their food joy. In addition to life in the kitchen, she holds a bachelor's degree in journalism and communications from Averett University and is a creative director, writer and frequent contributor to regional media, including television. For over a decade, Amy has been an Outer Banks restaurant advice columnist and has had columns featured in the *Outer Banks Voice* and the *Virginian-Pilot's* Coast OBX. She has been the lead food writer for *Outer Banks Magazine* since its inception in 2012. She was the founder and owner of Outer Banks Epicurean Inc., a culinary adventure business she began in 2005 that offered cooking lessons, food tours, team building experiences and private chef services. Amy teaches that eating is a lifestyle choice and in her classes she shares her enthusiasm for slow foods, ingredient exploration, flavor profile combinations and artful meal presentations. She now owns and operates an artisan, hand-harvested sea salt business called Outer Banks SeaSalt. Originally from Jackson, Michigan, Amy has lived, worked and shopped for groceries on the Outer Banks since 1986. Amy is an advocate for feel good food, a community connector and a supporter of local resources. The pragmatic optimist lives with her husband, John, and their dog, Vida, in the coastal country community of Poplar Branch, North Carolina, just over the Wright Memorial Bridge from the Outer Banks.

Visit us at
www.historypress.com
....